A Visitor's Guide to the

TEXAS COASTAL BEND

DINAH BOWMAN

Marilyn Bennett

Illustrated by Dinah Bowman

EAKIN PRESS ★ **Austin, Texas**

FIRST EDITION

Copyright © 1991
By Marilyn Bennett

Published in the United States of America
By Eakin Press
An Imprint of Sunbelt Media, Inc.
P.O. Drawer 90159 ★ Austin, TX 78709-0159

ISBN 0-89015-834-7

Library of Congress Cataloging-in-Publication Data

Contents

Acknowledgments

Several years ago, Dinah came to my classroom of first graders to teach them the process of Gyotaku, the art of fish printing. Her daughter was in my classroom at the time. The experience was so enjoyable for the children that I wrote an article about it for the *Early Childhood Teacher Magazine* (Fall/Winter 1988). It was during this time that we began to develop a friendship and discovered a mutual interest in developing a tourguide for the area in which we live. We formed a team with myself as author and Dinah as illustrator. Much of our research has been a joint effort. Dinah has contributed over 200 illustrations. My job of writing has been both challenging and fun. After two years of researching and writing about this unique area of Texas we give you *A Visitor's Guide to the Texas Coastal Bend*.

We applaud the early settlers of the Texas coast that endured unbelievable hardships with stoic determination and a will to survive. We are also indebted to the many others who have contributed their ideas, their help, and their encouragement to this book. First of all, we thank our typists LaRue Goldsmith and Ruth Mimms for the enormous task of typing the final copies of this book and their continued mental support and enthusiasm. Throughout this undertaking, we have been blessed with individuals who took the time and effort to write letters with valuable historical information about their particular area: Elinore Stewart of Three Rivers, J. C. Crews of Kenedy, and Bobbi J. Luker, of Weesatche. We are grateful to Jane Deisler, curator of the Corpus Christi Museum, for opening the Museum Library to us and assisting our research. Gene Blacklock, curator of the Welder Wildlife Refuge, helped compile the flower checklist. Ginny McCullough, reference librarian of the Portland Library, gave us research assistance. From Odem we met the delightful Della Mae Baylor, who provided us with old maps, information, and infectious resolve to complete this book. Our good friends Pam and Clay Clark unselfishly took their place as our Xerox King and Queen! Special appreciation must be given to Pam and Ron Jorgensen, computer experts, for their tireless patience with the author! We are thankful for Savannah Robinson, kind proofreader, supporter of our project, a great resource. Photographers Mike Morgan and particularly Richard Siemens of the Rockport *Herald*, helped tremendously. The Corpus Christi Area Convention and Visitors Bureau communications manager, Judy Ramos, was most kind and helpful with photographs as well. Eakin Publication's production manager, Tom Hayes, has been a helpful blessing with his calm and positive assurances. Area Chambers of Commerce and history-oriented postmasters in small towns spent many hours with us on the telephone providing us with much of the colorful history of this area. Their knowledge about great, near great, and not so great events and people added much to the accuracy of this guide.

Had we not tackled this project we would never have had the pleasure of meeting many of these people. Their willingness to assist in any way was a blessing to both of us!

This book is lovingly dedicated to our husbands for their belief in us, our children for their love and patience, and most especially to our publisher, Edwin M. Eakin, mentor, editor, and friend. We thank you.

MARILYN BENNETT
DINAH BOWMAN

I

Alphabetical Listing of Towns

ALICE

Alice, Texas, has had a variety of names. It began with the Chisholm Trail passing through it. Shortly after 1850, a few settlers arrived in oxcarts and wagons. Their goal was to build a general store and found a trading center just east of present day Alice. The community bore the name of "Collins," after Mr. N. G. Collins, an extensive landowner in this section. The town of Collins was shortlived, lasting about 30 years, and became a ghost town. The San Antonio and Aransas Pass Railroad, wishing to push their rails south from San Antonio toward the Rio Grande, attempted to purchase right-of-way acreage through the village. Often being refused by some landowners, they secured tracksite approximately two miles to the west. In 1886, their line was completed to intersect with the Tex Mex tracks. A new town was started at the intersection where the two railroads met. It was called Bandana. The name Bandana was soon discarded in favor of the

Alice — Municipal Golf Course

new name, "Kleberg," honoring Mr. Robert J. Kleberg of the King Ranch; he was active in developing the area. Postal authorities refused to sanction the name of "Kleberg" because another community already bore the name. At the suggestion of Mr. Kleberg, the little town was named "Alice" in honor of his wife, Alice King. Alice was granted a Post Office August 22, 1888. Farming is one of Alice's greatest assets, producing primarily sorghum and cotton.

Points of Interest: South Texas Museum — Houses tools, antiques, records, documents and pictures and historical interest in the history of South Texas. Tues.–Fri. 1–5 P.M., 66 South Wright St.

Lone Star Flag — originated here. Sara Bradley Dodson, of Kentucky, wife of Texas patriot Archelaus Bynum Dodson, made the first flag for her husband's company. It was red, white, and blue with a single star. It flew at "Washington-on-the-Brazos" when the Declaration of Independence was signed March 2, 1836.

Hostilities with Mexico broke out on September 19, 1835, and the Harrisburg Company was one of the first to organize, marching under this flag designed by the wife of one of the company's leaders. It was blue, white and red with a white star on the field of blue.

Lake Alice — 5 minutes away, located on the north side of Alice in the city limits. Fishing, overnight camping, picnic area available.

Alice cement water tower — This is the largest concrete tower in the world.

Annual Events: Festival Bandana — Held in May. A mixture of Mexican/American cultures in music, food, and entertainment events.

Youth Rodeo — June — (512) 664-0401 — On Jim Wells County Fairgrounds.

Menudo Cookoff — July — (512) 664-0931 — At Knights of Columbus Hall.

Jim Wells County Fair — October — Country fun on fairgrounds. Queen's contest, carnival, booths, and exhibits, chili cookoff. (512) 664-8795.

AGUA DULCE

Agua Dulce was named for the sweet water that once flowed there. It is located on the highway between Banquette and Alice. Agua Dulce provides an excellent photographic backdrop of old buildings.

Agua Dulce — sunny day

Alfred — friendly neighbors

4

ALFRED

Alfred was originally named Driscoll. The town began in 1888 when the railroads arrived. In 1972 twenty people called Alfred home, but there's no guarantee they are still there.

ARANSAS PASS

This coastal town originated in 1909 with a land lottery. Tickets were sold for $100 apiece. It was the last known land lottery in the United States and was crashed by United States postal authorities! Aransas Pass borders some of the state's best salt water sport and commercial fishing grounds. It lies 21 miles northeast of Corpus Christi. Aransas was named for the pass between Mustang and St. Joseph Islands 6 miles off the coast of the city. The word "Aransas" originated from Nuestra Senora de Aranzazu — Our Lady of Aranzazu, a shrine in Spain. It is the home for hundreds of shrimp trawlers which fish the Gulf of Mexico and have earned for the city the appropriate title "Shrimp Capital of Texas." A giant shrimp across from the Chamber of Commerce celebrates the title.

Points of Interest: Conn Brown Harbor — This harbor is the largest and most modern shrimping facility in the world.

Seaman's Memorial Tower — dedicated to those who have lost their lives at sea. It is located on the point of the southern end of Conn Brown Harbor.

Conn Brown Harbor Park — located just south of Conn Brown Harbor.

Fishing — Unexcelled sport fishing.

Annual Events: Shrimporee — September — Shrimp capital of the world entertains visitors with three days of live entertainment, children's area, features shrimp, shrimp, and

5

Aransas Pass — shrimp boats
— Photo by Richard Siemens

more shrimp; at Roosevelt Stadium. Fri & Sat: Arts & Crafts. Sat: Parade, popular outhouse races, beauty contest, shrimp-eating contest. Sun: Men's sexy-legs contest. (512) 758-3713.

Blessing of the Fleet — Fourth of July in Conn Brown Harbor.

Taste of Aransas Pass — April — showcase of all local merchants.

AUSTWELL

Named for Preston Rose Austin and one of his partners, Jesse McDowell. Platted in 1912.

Austwell — Aransas National Wildlife Refuge
— Photo by Richard Siemens

Hay baling time at Banquete

BANQUETE

Banquete was a well-known watering hole on the Civil War Road between the Confederate States and Mexico. It was fed by the Agua Dulce Creek and Banquete Creek both, flowing from Mathis. Due to changes in present day agricultural methods, both creeks are typically dry. Today water wells are used.

BAYSIDE

Tiny but intriguing community spread along a bluff over Copano Bay. Close by is the ghost town of Old Copano, which Spain established in the mid-1700s as a port of supply for the mission, Presidio La Bahia, north of Goliad.

Points of Interest: St. Mary's Cemetery — This is a well-kept cemetery with some quite old dates, lovely inscrip-

Bayside

— Photo by Richard Siemens

tions, and attractive carvings, for rubbings.

Crofutt's Bakery — Delicious breads and pastries available here at quite reasonable prices.

Bayside Express — fresh seafood.

BEEVILLE

Nestled in the heart of the Coastal Bend Area, Beeville's climate allows visitors free reign in outdoor activities year-round. It is located 65 miles north of Corpus Christi.

In 1834 it was settled by Irish colonists. A boat from Ireland bearing 16 or 18 families arrived at Copano Bay. Among these families were the two original Heffernan families. The early settlers were constantly fearful of attack by Indians or Mexican banditos with good reason. The country was still a wilderness but wild game, including deer and turkey, were

9

Beeville

plentiful. Pasture land was excellent for stock. Bee County was named by Gen. Hamilton P. Bee. While he was Speaker of the House of Representatives, he asked that the new county  be named in memory of his father, Col. Bernard E. Bee. Colonel Bee was an attorney from South Carolina, as well as secretary of war under President Houston and secretary of state under President Lamar. Later he was minister of the U.S. from the Republic of Texas. Another native Southerner, G. W. McClanahan, operated the first mercantile business in town. He contributed much to the development of Beeville as storekeeper, farmer and gardener, deputy clerk, lodge keeper, postmaster, school teacher, Sunday School superintendent, and was active in the Masonic Lodge. His first store building was purchased by the Historical Society in 1962. It is open to the public.

Historical Tour: The Beeville Historical Society provides

a brochure for interested parties. It contains the following information on the homes:

Beeville on the Poesta: Marker on Courthouse Lawn.

Mexico granted land in 1834 to Ann Burke and James Heffernan. Mrs. Burke arrived as a widow following her husband's shipboard death of cholera. Long before these grants, savage Indians roamed this valley at will. The colony of the first settlers, although successful at first, soon met disaster. In 1836, James Heffernan, his brother John, and John Ryan, who had planned to join Texas patriots at Goliad, were planting a crop in a field at this site when they were massacred by Comanches. Also killed were James' family in his picket house upcreek. Beeville was originally called "Maryville" for Mary Heffernan (relative of those killed in 1836).

Cook Home: Built by John Cook. He was born in 1846 in a Texas-bound wagon train. At 17, he was a soldier in the Civil War. In 1866 he married Francis Miller. They lived in a rock house near this site. With son, R. J., they contributed much to the area cattle industry with the importation and breeding of fine registered Herefords. The house was erected in 1897 of select long-leaf pine. It was placed on the site to catch gulf breezes. Each room opens onto a porch. The house also has four fireplaces with solid wood mantels of mahogany, maple, oak. The architectural style is Victorian. It has been owned by William D. Dugat and family since 1941.

 Jim Little Homestead: $4^1/2$ miles west of Beeville on Cadiz Road. On F9 Ranch, the homestead was granted to the Littles in 1873, but was grazed earlier by his cattle. The Little home was built about 1870 of cypress and heart pine that was imported by steamer from Florida to Saint Mary's, then by ox-cart to the site. A kiln on the ranch was the source for the caliche blocks for the chimneys. The homestead has a good water well. A country store made this a campsite for early travelers such as Mexican horse traders. The homestead was a stage stop on the San Antonio-Brownsville Road until the railroad came into the area in 1886.

First Brick Building on Square: 108 W. Corpus Christi,

Beeville — vintage storefront

Beeville — 1891 storefront

Beeville — old-time "fillin' station"

Beeville. Victorian architecture. It was built in 1892 by grocer J. C. Thompson of brick from the Calavaros kiln near Elmendorf. In 1892 the upstairs of the building was the law office of Lon C. Hill, who later founded Harlingen. Afterward the second floor was used as the "Beeville Light Guard" armory.

Evergreen Cemetery: Block bounded by Bowie, Polk, Heffernan and Filmore Sts., Beeville. Land was first donated for the cemetery in 1859 by Ann Burke. In 1862 and 1872 additional land was purchased. It was restored in 1970.

The Camp-Ezell House: 1313 W. Flournay, Beeville. A fine example of a settler's "box" home, board-and-batten construction. The lumber is Florida long-leaf pine from a house torn down in Old Saint Mary's by Robert A. Ezell. The house has three chimneys; one served as the flue for the dining room fireplace and kitchen stove. Food was prepared on both. Ezell (1845–1936), a stonemason, built at this creek site in 1892.

George Home: 801 N. Adams, Beeville. Built in 1890 by Will H. and Julia George of materials from an early house on land inherited from her father, Major J. H. Wood (Texas cattle empire builder) who came from New York to join the Texas War for Independence. Remodeled in 1900, the house is raised cottage architecture and has elegantly detailed interior woodwork. Many social and cultural functions were held here at turn of century. Present owner is Mrs. Mary M. Welder, a Wood descendant.

Early Trails in Bee County: In Roadside Park on U.S. 181, 3.6 miles north of Beeville. From pack trails and wagon roads that marked this area have developed such modern roads as U.S. Highway 181. The old trails of In-  dians, wild cattle and Mustang horses formed highways for 17th, 18th, and 19th century expeditions coming from Mexico to claim sovereignty over land in Texas. Pioneers established towns along these old pathways. Beeville, the county seat, was situated at the natural intersection of San Patricio-Helena Road with Goliad-Laredo Road. About 20 miles south, the

Matamoros-Goliad Road (Camino Real to oldtimers) was probably the most historic road in this area. In the years 1861–1865 the "Cotton Road," called "lifeline of the Southern Confederacy," crossed Bee County. Thousands of Longhorns were driven north from the Rio Grande to the Red River and up the Dodge City Trail of the Chisholm Trail to northern markets. In this area were also La Pera (or grapevine) Road, the Indianola-Papalote Road, and a road to now-vanished Saint Mary's, a port on Copano, off the Gulf of Mexico.

Captain A. C. Jones: Confederate Marker in Roadside Park on U.S. 181, 3.6 miles north of Beeville. Captain Jones was one of the builders of the Southwest. He was a cattleman, served as sheriff of Goliad County in 1858–1860, fought in Civil War Cavalry and fought at Palmito Hill. Palmito Hill was the war's last battle 34 days after the surrender of Gen. Robert E. Lee. In 1886 he raised $75,000 to build S.A.&A.P. Railroad from San Antonio to Beeville. He was instrumental in getting G.H.&S.A. to extend a rail line from Victoria here in 1890. In his spare time he was county treasurer, a banker, and the president and general manager of Beeville Oil Mill!

McClanahan House: Between Jail and Library, 200 Block E. Corpus Christi, Beeville. It is the oldest business structure in Beeville. This edifice was erected about 1867 on east side of Courthouse Square, near Poesta Creek. It has served as a general store, lodging house, and post office. The architecture is pioneer western style, with southern porches. Built by G. W. McClanahan, Beeville's first merchant, who also owned the cemetery site.

Medio Creek: On U.S. 59 east of Beeville. It was named by the Spaniards about 1800 because of its midway position between the San Antonio and Nueces Rivers. The creek rises in Karnes County and empties into the Mission River. It has been crossed by explorers, padres, soldiers, and settlers who traveled on the early ox-cart roads that led from Mexico to Mission La Bahia at Goliad. The Cart War of 1857 was the first international rate dispute between Mexican and Texan carters. It began when the Mexicans dropped their rates and the Texans retaliated. It took place between Texas and Mexican teamsters on the freight route between San Antonio and

14

Gulf roads. The Mexican cart drivers used Mesquite beans as feed for their teams. Their refuse started the Mesquite brush which thrives along the creek. Early settlers were attracted here by the tall grass. Many veterans of the Texas Revolution were given bounty lands in the area to settle. The first post office in Bee County was established in 1857 at Medio Hill pioneer community, once a settlement further down the creek. In 1909, the town of Candlish was founded near here. It had a hotel, general store, and a school. When the store closed, Candlish became a ghost town. In 1938–1939, on Medio and Blanco Creeks, fossil beds yielded 1,000,000-year-old fossils of a new mastodon species (named Buckner's Mastodon), rhinoceros, elephants, alligators, camels and three-toed horses.

St. Philip's Episcopal Church: 311 E. Corpus Christi, Beeville. The transept was built in 1893 on this site originally purchased in 1890 for the heirs of G. W. McClanahan. In 1910, the nave was added with funds from the sale of a block of land given to the Missionary Jurisdiction of Western Texas by English-born H. W. Wilson, 1888. Early members donated furnishings, bell tower, and in 1896 an inscribed memorial bell. The first Protestant parochial school in the county was organized here in 1954. The Gothic design was retained in a 1964 renovation.

Gentry Duget: Grave marker in Mineral Cemetery. Gentry Duget was a colorful historian, orator, and journalist. Born on a nearby ranch, he was the son of Alex and Martha (Page) Duget. He earned his Law Degree, worked on seven Texas newspapers, and edited the *Cotton Ginner's Journal*. In 1958 he organized and chartered the Bee County Historical Commission.

The A. C. Jones Home: 611 E. Jones, Beeville. Built 1906 by Mrs. Jane Field Jones (1842–1918), philanthropist, builder of a local school and teacherage, and widow of "The Father of Beeville," Captain A. C. Jones. The home was occupied from 1918 to 1966 by Mr. and Mrs. Allen Carter Jones II. The home is still the property of her descendants. The house is early 20th century Baroque architecture with large formal rooms, 8 fireplaces, hardwood floors and high ceilings. It has been the site for entertainment of many Texas leaders, including governors. It is now owned by Mr. and Mrs. Edward Wicker.

Hunting — Area abounds with wild deer, dove, quail, turkey, and javelinas.

Bee County College — Offers advanced study and training through academic and vocational technical courses.

Naval Air Station — Located at Chase Field, it serves as a training station for pilots and has been a primary factor in the economic development and growth of the city.

Beeville Art Gallery and Museum — Art and craft displays. Museum gift shop offers antiques, collectibles. Open Tues, Thurs, Sat, Sun, 1–5 P.M., 401 E. Fannin St.

Annual Events: Diez y Seis de Septiembre — September — People gather to celebrate the true essence of Mexican culture with mariachis, authentic Mexican cuisine, and festive dancing.

Western Week — October — Bee County Coliseum and Rodeo Arena.

BERCLAIR

Berclair

Berclair is in the news, folks! President George Bush has hunted here for the last 20 years. He enjoys quail hunting every winter and the folks around here look forward to it. They say Mr. President is a great hunter and friendly to everyone. Their only complaint is that Beeville gets the news coverage.

17

Bishop — Texas speedster!

A rural center rich in cotton and grain. Bishop was a pre-planned town. In 1910, a complete power and sewerage system was installed, all streets were graded, complete with sidewalks, before the first town lot was offered for sale.

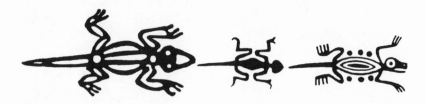

BLOOMINGTON

Bloomington — plenty of nectar

Dairy Queen Outpost.

CORPUS CHRISTI

Corpus Christi is truly the unsung gem of the Texas Coast. In addition to its swaying palm trees, scenic shoreline, and comfortable climate, it has a rich and colorful history as well as a promising future. Translated from Latin, Corpus Christi means "body of Christ." The city reportedly received its name from the Spanish explorer Alonzo Alvarez de Pineda. He discovered the area in 1519. If one cares to look a bit, there's an abundance of culture and entertainment here.

Points of Interest: Art Museum of South Texas — 1902 N. Shoreline. The museum was designed by nationally known architect Philip Johnson. Severely modern in design, this mu-

Corpus Christi — beautiful T-heads
— Photo by Richard Siemens

Corpus Christi — a visitors haven
— Photo by Richard Siemens

seum secures major exhibits on loan regularly, well worth seeing. Has a museum shop.

Art Community Center — 100 N. Shoreline — (512) 884-6406 — The Art Community Center is composed of seven art clubs. It serves all of South Texas with opportunities for local artists to show their work. Exhibits are changed monthly. The Little Gallery features individual artists monthly. Has a gift shop, tea room, and studios for artists in residence. Holds workshops and demonstrations by well-known artists from all over the country. It has an open air courtyard with a lovely view of the L-Head.

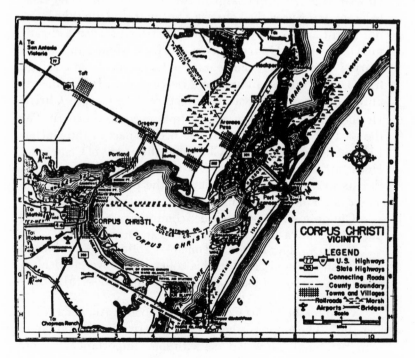

Bayfront Plaza Auditorium — N. end of Shoreline Blvd. Three levels feature changing exhibits of a myriad of interests. Auditorium seats 2,500.

C-Sculpture — Sculptors have a fantastic opportunity to release their creative urges and win prizes. Spectators will delight in the sights at the J. P. Luby Youth Park on Padre Island. Teams of participants compete to create the largest, most elaborate and original entries, beginning as early as dawn. For registration information call sponsor KNCN at (512) 289-1000. Day-long entertainment, free admission.

Centennial House — 411 North Broadway — Wed. 2–5. Special tours may be arranged for groups of 10 or more by calling (512) 992-6003 a week in advance — $2 for adults, $1 for students, under six free. The Centennial House is the oldest existing structure in the Corpus Christi area. It was built of "shell-crete" construction in 1849. Its history is rich and colorful. Prior to the Civil War the house belonged to a Mr. Howell, who left it in charge of two aged servants. The Confederate Army used the house as a hospital, and after the bombardment and seizure of Corpus Christi, it served as headquarters for the Quartermaster Corps stationed in Corpus Christi. Throughout the years, the house has been a refuge from Indian raids, banditos, and fierce storms. It is a fine example of Classic Revival Architecture. The Corpus Christi Heritage Society presents a Christmas event as a benefit. For the past few years, the event has been a part of the Harbor Lights celebration. During Christmas the rooms of Centennial House are decorated by local Garden Club members and area florists in a manner appropriate to the period of the house. There is a Yuletide shop in conjunction with the event.

Children's Park — Unique, community built waterfront park. At Cole Park, downtown on Ocean Drive.

Co-op — The Personal Touch — antique charm blends with fresh arts and crafts in this collection of over 40 dealers housed in one lovely location. 422 N. Chaparral — (512) 884-8522.

Corpus Christi Art Connection — 3636 S. Alameda (512) 854-1057. The emphasis here is on western wildlife and landscape art. Small but well done, with some important artists on their lists.

Corpus Christi Botanical Gardens — Wednesday–Sunday. Closed Thanksgiving, Christmas, and New Year's. Open Memorial Day and Labor Day. Hours 9:00 A.M. to 5:00 P.M. Admission charge. Enjoy the wild beauty of South Texas by walking a mesquite trail cut through a 30-acre remnant of virgin mesquite brush between the lake and Oso Creek. You can view more than 30 species of woody trees, shrubs, and subshrubs; six species of cactus; and many herbs and grasses. Peak blooming time is during spring and fall months. Others bloom all year. Stay on  the path and watch for snakes. "Take only pictures and leave only your footprints." Call (512) 852-2100 for a guided tour book available in the gift shop. Preliminary Gardens display many of the domestic and wild plants grown locally. Special collections include Hibiscus, Azalea, Banana, Aloe, Succulents, and Native Plants.

Corpus Christi Greyhound Races — 5302 Leopard — (512) 888-4385 — 7 days a week, evening and afternoon matinees. Grandstand admission, $1 adults, children under twelve free, admission to the clubhouse, $2.

Corpus Christi Marina — Located between Furman and Bayfront Arts and Sciences Park, on the Seawall. Always open. Three manmade islands dock sailboats, shrimpboats, party and fishing boats, and yachts. The T-heads and L-heads offer restaurants, jet skiing, paddle boating, skating, and interesting moorings such as the *Celika S.*, a beautiful yacht once owned by Al Capone.

Corpus Christi Museum — The museum recently expanded to include two new permanent exhibits, Shipwreck! and History of Naval Aviation Training. The museum features natural history, marine science and anthropology. Open 10–5 Tuesday–Saturday; Sunday 2–5. Admission $2 adults, children 50 cents in Arts & Science Park.

Corpus Christi Symphony — Provides several major concerts a year with renowned artists.

Corpus Christi Water Garden — Located in close proximity to the Corpus Christi Museum and the Art Museum. May be seen from the Harbor Bridge as well. The water garden is a lovely circular fountain that is a relaxing spot to pause and enjoy the scenic bay while sightseeing the nearby heritage park, art gallery, and museum. It has become a favorite photography spot for weddings and special events.

Downtown Gallery — 823 N. Water Street — Co-op of Coastal Bend artists & craftsmen exhibiting a wide range of local and state talent. Tues.–Sat., 8–5 & Sun. 12–4 P.M.

Hans Suter Park — Ennis Joslin Road — World famous bird watching.

Harbor Playhouse — This community theatre has something to offer everyone, from hilarious comedies and heart-rending dramas to toe-tapping musicals. It produces season after season of fine entertainment. 1 Bayfront Plaza. Productions all year long. Mainstage plays throughout the season and summer melodramas during a two-month mini season. Tickets: (512) 882-3356. Office: (512) 888-7469.

Heritage Park — Turn of century homes. 1600 N. Chaparral. This walking tour comprises nine restored homes situated on one square block facing Chaparral Street and bordered by Fitzgerald, Hughes, and Mesquite streets. All the homes have been restored by non-profit organizations with the exception of the Galvan house, which is owned and operated by the City of Corpus Christi. Tours may be arranged by calling the Multicultural Center, (512) 883-0639. They will also provide you with a map of the park detailing where each house is located and information about them. Following is a brief description of each house in the park which is provided by their brochure.

Lichtenstein House — #1 Heritage Park — (512) 888-5692. Monday through Friday — noon to 4:00 P.M. Julius Lichtenstein, son of the founder of Lichtenstein's Department Store, built this house in 1905. He and his wife Carrie Weil Lichtenstein lived in this home until 1913 and retained ownership until 1926. Simple in detail and scale, it is a Colonial Revival house. The turret clerestory windows are typical of Victorian Period architecture.

Sidbury House — #2 Heritage Park — (512) 883-9351. Tuesday through Thursday — 9:30 A.M. to 12:30 P.M. This home was built in 1893 by Charlotte Cook Scott Sidbury, bank director, lumber company manager and civic leader. It was one of twin houses built as rental properties and was never occupied by Mrs. Sidbury. It is the only remaining example of High Victorian architecture in Corpus Christi. This first floor is furnished as a Victorian home and has on display a marble top Jenny Lind table, c. 1850, a Steinway piano, c. 1893, and an Eastlake Style dining table and chairs, c. 1870. The Junior League, which restored the house in 1977, has its offices on the second floor. The asymmetrical Victorian structure has all the elements of the Queen Anne Style including irregular outlines, verandas, balconies and steep-pitched roofs. The gingerbread look is due to delicate and elaborate woodwork on the porches. The moorish arch over the front steps and the fan-shaped eave brackets are the most distinctive features of the house.

Gugenheim House — #3 Heritage Park (512) 887-1601 — Monday through Friday 10 A.M. to 4 P.M. In 1882, Simon Gugenheim arrived in Corpus Christi with $40. He became a successful business man and helped the city's economy during the 1893 recession. He and his wife, Lila Belle, built this house in 1905. Camp Fire, Inc. moved the house to its present site and restored it. The front rooms are furnished in the style of the 1900s. This is the only square turreted structure remaining in Corpus Christi. The tri-faceted porch, spanning gabled wings, and the gingerbread details are typical of the Late Victorian Period.

Littles-Martin House — #4 Heritage Park (512) 884-8541 — Monday through Friday 10 A.M. to 4 P.M. Hattie Moore Littles is believed to have been one of the first Black natives of Corpus Christi. She and her husband Willis worked for rancher John G. Kenedy and in 1915 were confirmed Catholics. John G. and Marie Stella Kenedy were their godparents. Hattie and Willis worked for many prominent families in Corpus Christi. When the Littles retired, the Kenedys gave them this house. Its original site is unknown, but it was moved to North Staples Street about 1918. The Littles' daughter, Mary Beth Littles Martin, taught piano in the home for many years and lived there until her death in 1983. It was restored in 1986 by the National Association for the Advancement of Colored People (NAACP) to serve as their offices. The front rooms contain period furnishings and exhibits on Black history. The fireplace mantle is carved from Tigerwood, commonly known as "Nigerian walnut," and native to West Africa. The front is hand-carved pine. The beveled wood siding, hip roof with projecting gable and chamfered bay suggest Queen Anne Victorian Cottage architecture. Decorative features include shingles on the facade between windows and roofline and a small window in the gable.

Galvan House — #5 Heritage Park — (512) 883-0639 — Monday through Friday 10–4 Saturday 10 A.M. to 2 P.M. This house was built from a design by Francis Garrett French, wife of A. M. French. They had the house built in 1908 to accommodate both family and friends. French was a surveyor on the construction of the Tex-Mex Railroad, an attorney and founder of the First State Bank. He also founded and directed the first abstract title company in Corpus Christi. In 1942, Rafael Galvan purchased the house and it stayed in his family until 1982. Galvan came to Corpus Christi in 1896, worked as a fisherman and then became Corpus Christi's first Mexican-American police officer. The Galvan House serves as headquarters for the Multi-cultural Center. The grounds include a carriage house and courtyards. The Colonial Revival architecture is formal in appearance due to the classic columns on two levels. Beveled glass in the front doors and sidelights has one and one-half inch bevels, much larger than usual.

Grande-Grossman House — #6 Heritage Park — (512) 883-5134 — Monday through Friday 10 A.M. to noon & 1 P.M. to 4 P.M. The Grande men were entrepreneurs who owned the Ben Grande Saloon, one of the largest and last old-time cantinas in Texas. Benito (Ben) Grande was born in 1862 and came to Corpus Christi with his family in the late 1870s. Ben succeeded his father in operating family businesses, became a leader in the community. He built this house on Artesian Street in 1907. The Grossman family began emigrating from Russia in the early 1900s. Ed, Henry, Simon and their sister Ida Grossman opened a department store next door to this house. It was restored by the LULAC Council in 1985. It serves as offices for the LULAC National Educational Service Center. Revisions to the house have changed the style from Victorian to Craftsman with elements of Prairie architecture. Dominant features include the stick style eave brackets and brick piers.

Merriman-Bobys House — #7 Heritage Park — (512) 883-2787 — Monday through Friday 10 A.M. to 2 P.M. — This is the second-oldest structure existing in Corpus Christi. (The oldest is Centennial House, 411 North Upper Broadway.) It was built in 1851 by Walter Merriman, a lawyer and land developer. During the Civil War and the 1867 yellow fever epidemic, the house was used as a hospital. Nearly one-third of the population, including Corpus Christi's only three doctors, died in the epidemic. The house had many owners over the years, including prominent ranchers who used it as a town home. Mr. & Mrs. Ernest Bobys purchased the house in 1936 and the local chapter of the Texas Poetry Society held meetings here. In 1981, Morris Lichtenstein bought the house and donated it to the city. This is probably the most unique structure in the Park, yet the most typical of early Corpus Christi architecture. The open porch and shellcrete fireplaces are good examples of Early Texas regional architecture. The distinctive three gables are results of additions to the original structure, which was built with native wood and square nails. The front entry includes a raised panel door bordered by sidelights and a full transom. It now houses the Corpus Christi Arts Council.

Jalufka House — Czech Heritage Society — Restoration in progress — The Jalufka House was built in 1901 by James L. Jalufka at 1408 N. Mesquite in what is known as "Old Irishtown." The father of James Jalufka was originally from Moravia in Austria (present day Czechoslovakia) and immigrated to the United States at the age of seventeen. He later became a citizen of the United States. James Jalufka attended West Point and later built the house on the lot where he and his wife, Helen J. "Captain," maintained an outstanding rose garden. The house was restored by the Czech Heritage Society of South Texas for offices, meeting rooms, a History and Genealogy Research Library and a photo gallery of South Texas Czech pioneers. Unusual paired columns defining the front porch and a bay window are typical of Southern Bungalow architecture. The house is accented with gently pitched broad gables supported by knee braces. The foundation is a good example of rusticated blocks.

McCampbell House — Irish Cultural House, Inc. — Restoration in progress. Mary Alice Ward McCampbell, widow of Nueces County Attorney William Berry McCampbell, built this house about 1908 on Water Street, a few feet from Corpus Christi Bay. The seawall, which now protects downtown Corpus Christi from flood tides, was not completed until 1942. In 1919, a hurricane and its storm tides isolated residents of Old

Irishtown from the Bluff's high ground. Mary Ward Mc-Campbell and her three sons watched the storm from this house. As the tides rose, they fled to the second floor and watched the flood waters rise nearly level with the second story porch, over 20 feet above the street. They later recalled seeing entire houses, dead animals and debris flow past the porch. Early in 1920, Mary McCampbell died of pneumonia that her family said she contracted while standing watch on the porch during the storm. Her eldest son, William Ward, sold the house to his cousin in 1921. The Ionic Capitals, lattice enclosures and wraparound porches are typical of the Classic Revival architecture. It is being restored by the Irish Cultural House, Inc. for offices and meeting rooms.

Hummer/Bird celebration — Held each September, this festival features an array of quality speakers, field trips, boat trips, and booths. Call (512) 729-6445.

International Ballet Company — 3210 SPID Hall #4.

 International Kite Museum — Small but interesting museum traces the history of kites as they have been used in the Orient, Europe and the U.S., in science and warfare, as airplanes, and by Paul Garber, modern kite pioneer. This unique museum is on the grounds of the Best Western Sandy Shores Resort, Corpus Christi Beach. Open seven days a week, 10–5 daily. Free. (512) 883-7456. Kite Shoppe is enclosed in the museum and buyers may try their hand at kite flying right next door on the lovely Corpus Christi Beach, where the ocean breezes are always blowing.

Joseph A. Cain Memorial Art Gallery — Del Mar College — Baldwin & Ayers.

Lone Star Gallery — 4221 S. Alameda (512) 884-9333 — Mon.–Fri., 9 A.M.–5 P.M. A fine gallery dealing in bronzes, prints, wildlife cases.

Los Miradores Del Mar — "overlooking the sea" in Spanish. Eight miradores grace the bayfront along Shoreline Dr. Are a generous contribution from the Durrill Foundation. Each includes a brief account of the work our earliest explorers and are dedicated to a different historical event in Texas. Architectural design similar to those viewed in Mexico and

Morocco by the Durrills. It is well worth stopping to simply enjoy the view or to read the interesting accounts.

Melodrama — During the summer weekends, the Harbor Playhouse in Bayfront Arts & Science Park produces delightful and humorous melodramas and the popcorn to throw besides! Cabaret-style seating, food & drinks at tables. To reserve tickets, call Playhouse Box Office, (512) 882-3356. Curtains are at 8 P.M.

Museum of Oriental Cultures — Furman Plaza — (512) 883-1303. Monday through Friday 10–4, Sunday 2–5. Adults $1, children 25 cents. Collection includes hakata dolls, cultural and historical dioramas, porcelain, ceramics, textiles, bronze, and lacquerware.

Naval Air Station — Located at the end of Ocean Drive South. Bus tours Thursdays at 1 beginning at the north gate on Ocean Drive. (512) 939-2568. Free.

Oliver's Village Gallery — Alameda at Doddridge, in "The Village." (512) 855-0911 — Quality impressionist and contemporary artists. Collector prints featuring waterfowl and wildlife.

Ocean Drive — This lovely winding drive is lined with palm trees between the bay and luxurious homes. A beautiful, relaxing drive, stately and majestic homes promise to make this drive rival any in the United States. Passes several city parks including Oleander Park (sailboarding), Cole Park (fishing pier) and leads to the Hans Suter Park (bird watching).

Padre Island National Seashore — Via John F. Kennedy Causeway.

Paddlewheeler Flagship — Bay cruises, weekend jazz. People's Street T-head.

Planetarium — King High School, 5225 Gollihar. Program begins at 7:30 P.M. Small admission fee. Call the school for dates each summer.

Port of Corpus Christi — 222 Power (512) 882-5633. On any given day, this port is active with tankers coming and going. Vessels from all over the world sail here to move grain, cotton, oil, and chemicals. It was built in 1854. It is 45 feet deep. The safest way to view the port is from the free observation platform 235 feet below Harbor Bridge. Another way is via boat, and the most exciting way is by taking a careful walk along the pedestrian walkway on the Harbor Bridge. This is a beautiful, windy walk, but not if you're a sissy! Call the port office to see if any ships are allowing visitors.

Starlight Concerts — Each Sunday evening in the amphitheatre at Cole Park, 1400 Ocean Drive, near downtown. The open-air municipal band concerts generally include light classics, marches, and show tunes. Bring lawn chairs, blankets, or pillows when you come! Music begins at 8:30 P.M.

Supertrack Grande Prix — 3001 Seagull. (512) 884-7223.

Texas State Aquarium — at 800 N. Shoreline, 1200 N. Tower. (512) 881-8220. A marvelous educational, entertainment, and economic resource. It has been designated the "Official Aquarium of Texas" by the 69th Texas Legislature. Includes exhibits of estuarine and marine environment, ocean technology, and tropical coral reef. The Aquarium is committed to scientific study, informative presentation, and special care of the aquatic environment of the Gulf of Mexico and the Caribbean Sea. It is dedicated to the enhancement of today's world and the preservation of tomorrow's. Educational classes are provided as well as guest lecture programs, special film presentations, and possible travel excursions.

U.S.S. *Lexington* — United States largest aircraft carrier. Being converted to a museum. Will be berthed near the Texas State Aquarium. Admission fee.

Water Street Market — A charming little oasis in the middle of downtown Corpus Christi, this cluster of interesting shops and exceptional restaurants is a must for visitors and local yokels as well. Water Street Oyster Bar is one of the city's finest restaurants. A fresh seafood market is across the courtyard (Water Street Seafood Company) with a potpourri of specialty shops in between. Totally Texas is filled to the brim with Texana that can be read, worn, or eaten. Gifts by the Sea has a nautical atmosphere, and just around the corner is Che Bello's, a sidewalk cafe that offers gourmet sandwiches, sorbetto, or gelato for dessert, and espresso to top off your meal. Nearby, the Executive Surf Club serves burgers, nachos, live music and cold drinks. Tarasan's Gallery will invite you to stroll leisurely through hand painted clothing!

Corpus Christi — Watergarden

Corpus Christi — Aquarium

Harbor and Bay Tours: Trolley — Stops at bayfront hotels and downtown tourist sites and one of the malls. A great way to get a good look at Corpus Christi's marina, restaurants, and night spots downtown. Monday–Friday. 4:45 P.M.–9:45 P.M. every 30 minutes. Saturdays 11 A.M.–10:15 P.M. every 15 minutes. Fare 25 cents.

Capt. Clark's Bay and Harbor Sightseeing Cruises aboard the Flagship paddle-wheeler and the 250-passenger Gulf Clipper provide day and evening cruises along the bay. Both vessels available for private parties. (512) 883-1693.

Flagship — Gulf Clipper.

Fishing Charters: Back Bay Guide Service, Captain Clark, Star Trek, Sea Serpent.

Marina Activities:

Excursion Boats — Charter boats are docked at the People's Street T-Head or Cooper's Alley L-Head and are available for fishing and scenic trips.

Star Trek — takes 4-hour trips for bay fishing. Boat accommodates up to 85 passengers. (512) 883-5131 or (512) 991-3143.

Advantage Charters — provides private charters for excursion and deep-sea fishing. Half day and all day trips are available. All cruises are limited to a maximum of six persons. (512) 241-3993.

Coastal Bend Charters — Offers sailing cruises with a licensed guide. (512) 883-7245.

Dolphin Watch — Seasonal when dolphins are in the bay. Trips at 8 and 10 A.M. $10 per person — (512) 882-4126.

Charter Boat Associates — docked at the L-Head and provides captained charters and bareboat (no captain) charters. Captained charters can be 4-hour or 8-hour trips and bareboat charters are available for a minimum of 8 hours. (512) 881-8503.

International School of Sailing — Yacht Basin L-Head. (512) 881-8503.

Sailing and Sailboards: Charter Boat Association, Coastal Bend Charters, Optimistic Charter Service.

Sports-Recreational Equipment for Rent: Sailing, skiing, or windsurfing are no further than the local marina. Rental items are located at the People's Street T-Head.

Paddle 'N Fun — aqua cycles, paddle boats, sailboats and sailboards for rent. Some items can be rented for a half hour and others are available by the hour. Life jackets are included in the rental cost. Sailing and sailboard lessons at an hourly rate. Daily 10–sundown. (512) 854-8723.

C.C. Water Sports — jet skis and sailboats for rent. Skis by the half hour, boats by the hour for 1 or 2 people. Daily 10–6. (512) 850-7208.

Beach Boat Rentals — aqua cycles for your enjoyment. (512) 643-3749.

Surreys, Inc. — available for rent on the Shoreline seawall. Take a ride in these popular buggies with the fringe on the top and enjoy the bayfront from a different perspective. (512) 887-8717 or 887-8715.

Corpus Christi Water Taxi — one-way or round-trip service from the marina to McGee Beach, Corpus Christi Beach and other stops along the bayfront. (512) 882-4126.

Fishing Piers, Jetties, and Channels:

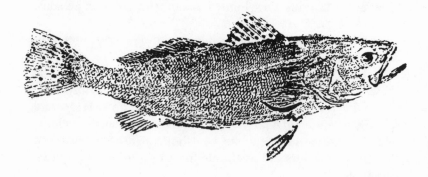

Breakwater Jetty — C.C. Bay Marina. Lighted, open 24 hours, free, concession. The T-Heads and 14' seawall that runs along Shoreline Blvd. are popular spots for fishermen.

Cole Park Pier — Corpus Christi on Ocean Drive. Lighted, open 24 hours, free.

Humble Channel — Under Humble Bridge on the way to Padre Island. Free.

Nueces Bay Pier — Corpus Christi Beach, Hull St. exit, wooden, lighted, open 24 hours, admission, concession.

Boat Launch Ramps:

Intercoastal Canal — Under JFK Bridge on Padre Island. Lawrence St. T-Head — C.C. Yacht Club Basin on Shore Blvd. Oso Bay — End of Ocean Drive. Admission. Concession. Rincon Road — Beneath the Nueces Bay Causeway.

Golf:

Public — Oso Beach Golf Course, 5600 S. Alameda. (512) 991-5351. 18 holes; 5,800 yards, par 70.

Gabe Lozano, Sr. Golf Center — 4401 Old Brownsville Road. (512) 883-3696. 18 holes, Par 72.

Pharaoh Country Club, 711 Pharaoh Dr. (512) 991-1490.

Windsurfing: Corpus Christi is the windsurfing capital of the world. The coastline's circular geography and flat, shallow waters have gained national attention in sailing and surfing publications. This sport is relatively new. It began in California in the 1960s. Some refer to it as sailboarding because it combines surfing and sail-  ing. One must employ the same skills as needed to navigate a sailboat or catamaran. Mild winter temperatures make this area ideal for this sport year-round. Lessons are available at local rental shops. Nice spots for families and beginners are Mud Hole in the Laguna Madre near the JFK Causeway, Bird Island Basin, located within Padre Island National Seashore. Experts frequent Oleander Park. Oleander Park is really the north end of Cole Park, and is the only city-sanctioned sailboard park in the world. It was adopted by the Corpus Christi Sailboard Association. Intermediate to expert sites are Corpus Christi Beach and the Oso Pier area. Corpus Christi Beach is located just over the Harbor Bridge and both north and south winds give windsurfers a real workout. Oso Pier is on Ocean Drive near Corpus Christi State University. The first ever Boardsailing Museum and Hall of Fame will open in the summer of '91 at the Cargo Dock One area of the Port of Corpus Christi.

Tennis — Municipal: H.E.B. Tennis Center — 1520 Shely (512) 888-5681; 24 courts, $1.50 days, $2.00 nights.

South Bluff Center — 502 King St. (512) 883-6942; 10 courts; $1.50 days, $2.00 nights.

Tennis — Private: C.C. Country Club
La Mirage Racquet & Athletic Club
Pharaoh's Country Club
Sheraton Marina Inn

Annual Events: Bayfest — End of September, first of October — This festival began as a bicentennial celebration, but has developed into a citywide event gaining popularity in the entire coastal bend region. The fest includes fireworks, a boat parade, a street parade, sailboat regatta, arts & crafts, foods, booths, Coast Guard sea-air rescue demonstration, and the "Anything-That-Can-Float-But-A-Boat" race. (512) 887-0868.

Buccaneer Days — Last week of April into May — Commemorates the landing of Alonza Alvares, explorer who discovered Corpus Christi. The "Buc Days" feature parades, fireworks display, continuous carnival, a sailboat regatta, sporting events, and music competitions.

"Art in the Heart of Corpus Christi" — a three-day art event, located downtown. (512) 882-3242.

New Year's Day 2-mile swim — (512) 880-3460 — C.C. Parks & Recreation. Held at Collier pool. The Parks also hold meets in February, March, October, and November.

Boar's Head and Yule Log Festival — January — First Christian Church (512) 883-1363 — A musical celebration of good triumphing over evil. Set in 13th century style and costume, this religious festival is presented annually. Each year the medieval costumes (handmade) are more beautiful than ever, with beefeaters, feathers, stockings, and much, much more. The Festival features no dialogue, but is all set to music. Presented on Epiphany Saturday and Sunday, 4 performances, no admission.

Waterfront Art Market — First and Third Sundays — People's Street T-Head (512) 880-3474.

Gulf Coast Antique Show — February and July — Bayfront Plaza — Admission, modern to antiques, (512) 882-6403.

R.V. Show — January — Held annually at Bayfront Plaza — (713) 589-7991.

Arts & Crafts — (512) 991-2438. Held in the Coliseum on the third Sundays of January, February, March, April, May, and October. Held on the second Sundays of November and December.

The Corpus Christi Kantorel — February — Variety of selections by choral ensemble of students and teachers at Warren Theatre at C.C.S.U. — (512) 994-2335.

Valentine's Day Arts and Crafts Show — Cullen Mall at Airline and Alameda. Shows in February, March, April, May, Christmas in July, September, October PreChristmas, November, and December. (512) 991-2236.

Auto Show — Held annually in February at the Convention Center — Sponsored by the C.C. Caller Times — (512) 883-8543.

South Texas Doll and Toy Show — February and July — (512) 547-3757. It is held at the convention center.

Rose Show — Padre-Staples Mall each spring and fall in April and November.

Texas Leisure Sports Expo — February — Convention Center — (512) 991-2999.

Gun Show — (512) 663-3218 — March and other times. Admission.

Custom Car and Hot Rod Show — Convention Center in

February each year. Model cars to 18 wheelers, go-carts, and show cars. (512) 887-0009.

Air Force Band — March — Free — Bayfront Plaza — (512) 884-2011.

Annual African Violet Show — March — Greeley Garden Center — (512) 992-4571.

Irish Parade — March — Starts at Courthouse on to Shoreline to Heritage Park and around McCampbell House — Refreshments served — (512) 888-4000.

Folklife Festival — March — Multicultural Center — (512) 883-0639.

Beach to Bay Marathon — May — annual relay for Junior High and Senior High students. Is 26.2 miles long, 6 people to a group, running 4.4 miles each. Held near Kennedy Causeway. Hold one on July 4th as well. (512) 993-5838.

Bird and Flower Tour — May — Three days of birding and plant-seeing in South Texas — (512) 993-9885.

Easter Egg Hunt — City-wide at South Bluff Park — Children 10–12 years free.

Fiesta Botanica Weekend — May — Dinner and Gala — food vendors, arts and crafts, entertainment — (512) 993-7551.

Naval Air Show and Open House — Each April and May at Naval Air Station (512) 939-2674.

Olympic Regatta — May — Hobie Cats — North Beach at Sandy Shores (512) 884-5892.

Corpus Christi Symphony — (512) 882-4091 — Seven concerts a year.

First Friday Uptown Art Event — (512) 883-1363 — Held at noon on the first Friday of each month in the first floor town center of the American Bank Plaza Building located at 711 N. Caranchua. Hosts local artists and performers as well.

Art Exhibition of Corpus Christi Exhibit — May — Local Artists exhibit (512) 994-0724.

U.S. Sailboard Open — May — Cole Park, Oleander Point — World Class Event (512) 884-2011.

Harbor Lights Celebration — This is the day in December when the mayor flips the switch and lights the many sailboat masts in the marina; Mr. & Mrs. Santa Claus appear.

Hunting and Fishing Show — (713) 589-7991 — Corpus Christi is located in the middle of the two largest hunting areas in Texas — the South Texas brush country and the Edwards Plateau area of the Hill Country. It is also on the coast of the Laguna Madre and Padre Island, the home of some of the finest trout and red fishing on the Texas coast. This annual show draws record crowds with fish-a-rama, stage shows, demonstrations, booths, and seminars.

Texas Jazz Festival — July — Free clinics, concerts, and festival cruises are rampant at this annual festival. A Jazz Mass is held Sunday morning and the rest of the day is filled with jazz from several stages surrounding the Water Garden at the north end of the bayfront. (512) 854-9634.

Corpus Christi Boat Show — January — (512) 991-0369.

Winterfest Travel Show — February — Travel extravaganza with exhibits from over 40 states and Canada; Winter Texans play host for their native states. Arts & crafts, live entertainment, health screenings, golf tournament, fishing tournament, catastrophic health seminar, doll show, square dancing, Texas-sized pot luck supper, and lots of good food. Also Kid's Korner with games, clowns and other funny characters. (512) 518-2597.

Gulf Coast Gem & Mineral Show — March — Bayfront Plaza Convention Center — competition in all classes, working exhibits, gem cutting, jewelry making, jade carvings, metal craft dealers, children's games, door prizes.

Texas Weapon Collectors Gun Show — (512) 663-3218 — held several times a year in the Bayfront Plaza Auditorium.

Naval Air Show & Open House — May — (512) 939-2674.

Ultimate Yacht Race — May — (folks from all over the world gear up for this new race) $1 million prize attracts yachtsmen from Germany, England, New Zealand and all across the U.S.; J-24 races with prize money going to top 10; endorsed by U.S. Yacht Racing Union; party spectator boats available for spectacular view of starting line.

Texas State Stamp Show — June — Texas' first World's Series of Philately Show. Includes 3,300 pages of displays by local, state and national exhibitions. Stamp and postal history exhibits from the U.S. Confederacy and foreign countries.

Sunday Night Band Concert — June — (512) 880-3460.

Corpus Christi Beach Party — June — (512) 880-3460.

Grayfest — July — Memorial Coliseum — third Saturday in July — (512) 528-2579 — admission.

Creative Arts Center ART/CAMP — July — (512) 888-5692.

Navy Regatta and Relief Festival — August — Picnic-style festivities at Naval Air Station, with most activity on Saturday. Keelboat, multihull, boardboat and sailboard races; kite show, Coast Guard auxillary exhibit and NOAA weather awareness booth. Foods and souvenirs available along seawall area. Military  Challenge Cup Race on Sun. Air Station open to visitors both days. (512) 939-2444 or 939-2425.

Ruff Riders Regatta — September — (512) 854-3375 — 150-mile race from Port Isabel to JFK Causeway.

End of Summer Arts & Crafts Show — September — (512) 991-2236 — Lots of arts, crafts, handmade items and plants at Cullen Mall.

Diez y Seis de Septiembre Celebration — September — Bayfront Convention Center — City's largest Mexican celebration features parade with bands, floats, mariachis, ballet folkorico, show cars and trucks, El Grito ceremony, and much more. (512) 882-3262, or 851-1414.

Navy Concert Band — November — (512) 884-2011.

YWCA Carousel of Arts and Crafts — November (512) 857-5661 — This is Corpus Christi's oldest Arts and Crafts

Fair. It has over 170 booths that exhibit a wide variety of high quality work; held at Memorial Coliseum. Has a special appeal for hunters' "widows" as it is held the opening weekend of hunting season every year. (512) 857-5661.

Corpus Christi Chorals — December — (512) 882-4091.

Christmas Floral Designers Showcase — December — Area florists lavishly decorate rooms of Centennial House, city's oldest structure; Yuletide Shop. Sponsored by the Heritage Society.

Christmas Tree Forest — (512) 884-3844 — Art Museum of South Texas transformed into a breathtaking forest of spectacularly decorated Christmas trees. It has included a tree with nothing but hundreds of seashells; another with finely crafted handmade dolls. (Closed Dec. 25 but reopens after Christmas.) (512) 884-3844 or 992-3948.

Trail Rides — A trail ride to San Antonio in conjunction with the livestock show in San Antonio. End of January, first of February.

AAUW Annual Book Sale — February — Padre Staples Mall — Includes silent auction and 29 different categories.

Greek Festival — November — St. Nicholas Church — 502 N. Chaparral Bazaar with Greek food, jewelry, arts & crafts (512) 883-9843.

Driscoll — Good buy!

DRISCOLL

Begun in 1904 when the St. Louis, Brownsville, and Mexican Railway building south from Robstown located a station on Robert Driscoll's ranch. Driscoll named the site after himself.

Robert Driscoll was a wealthy cattleman that was generous with his good fortune. By far his best gift to Texas was his lively daughter, Clara Driscoll. She became a legend for her notable contributions as an author, patriot, financier, and gifted stateswoman. Today Driscoll Children's Hospital provides free medical care for underprivileged children.

FALFURRIAS

Some say the Spanish meaning is "heart's delight." It possibly refers to some lovely local wildflower. This remote community is the county seat of Brooks County. In early 1800s the owners lived in Mexico and had ranch outposts in Falfurrias. The outposts failed under Indian attack. In the early 1900s, arrival of the railroad brought mail, which had come in by horseback, prior to that time. By 1908 a large creamery was introduced and grew to such an extent that by the 1920s Falfurrias, famous for its fine butter, was a household name.

Points of Interest: Heritage Museum — 300 N. St. Mary's — (512) 325-2907. Tuesday through Friday, 11–5. Free. Contains a special collection on the Texas Rangers, as well as collections pertaining to the founding and development of South Texas ranching.

Roadside Park — U.S. Hwy. 281 south eight miles. Always open, free. This lovely park is one of Texas' finest. This long stretch of flat country welcomes this little oasis, nestled in live oaks. It has shaded picnic tables and rest rooms.

Grave of Don Pedrito Jaramillo — famed curandero. (A curandero is a healer and is an ancient part of Mexican culture that is still in existence today. They feel their gift is from God and use natural remedies and potions made from herbs

Falfurrias — Don Pedrito Jaramillo

and teas.) Jaramillo was born in Jalisco, Mexico. He came to
Los Olmos Ranch in 1881. He was said to have been cured
through faith, then given the gift of healing in a vision. Many
came to him, because unlike other faith healers, he claimed no
power of his own, but said that God's healing was released
through faith. He did not charge for his services. Patients gave
or withheld as they chose. But whatever was given voluntarily
he often gave to the poor — food as well as remedies. He traveled widely to visit the sick. Hundreds gave testimonials of the
healings (1829–1907).

Annual Events: Watermelon Festival — June — First
Friday and Saturday. Located at the Falfurrias High School,
S. Henry Street. The festival highlights a seed spitting contest,
dance, parade, and watermelon eating contest. 50 cents admission is charged.

Fiesta del Campo — October — Continuous musical entertainment all three days at Lasater Park. Sat.; Trail Ride.
Sat. & Sun.; Softball tourney. Sun.; Golf tourney and chili
cookoff. (512) 325-3333 or 325-2860.

Fiesta Ranchera — May — Kiddie Park — Music, foods,
10-K Run, Softball & Golf Tourneys, Carne Guisada Contest.

Falfurrias Mexican Village — Second weekend in June — Rides, food, and crafts — (512) 325-2370.

Fourth of July — Rodeo demonstrations of vanishing skills, such as corn shelling, butter making, and quilting are included in the festivities.

Santa Comes to Town — Pioneer Park — first week of December (512) 325-3333.

Altar Society Bazaar — (512) 325-3333.

Falfurrias Four Seasons Bazaar — Second weekend in April — Catholic Church (512) 325-2918.

FANNIN

Located on Highway 59 between Goliad and Victoria, this modest community was named after James W. Fannin, a hero of the Texas Revolution. A state park marks the site of the Battle of Coleto Creek, March 19–20, 1836. After an in-

Fannin — Longhorn Steer

decisive delay at his Goliad fortress, Col. Fannin and his men were overtaken here by superior forces under General Urrea. Surrounded on an open plain, Fannin's 275 men fought off day-long assaults. However, they were forced to surrender to four-to-one odds. Col. Fannin was wounded. He was returned with his men to Goliad, where they were massacred. No camping facilities are available, but a picnic pavilion, water and restrooms are provided.

GEORGE WEST

Founded by Irish Catholics in the 1830s. Called "Fox Nation" for the Fox family; was renamed Gussettville in 1850s in honor of N. Gussett, owner of general store. Land for the town was donated by George West, a prominent rancher, after whom the town was named. It was typical of hundreds of

George West — Cattle

The Texas Longhorn

We pause here for a special note about Longhorn Steers. More than any other symbol, the Longhorn represents Texas. By 1860 a census recorded 31 million people and 26 million cattle in Texas. After the Civil War, Longhorns outnumbered people in Texas 9 to 1. However, by 1922, the magnificent breed was approaching extinction. The Texas Longhorn was nearer extinction than the buffalo or the whooping crane, when in 1927, the federal government appropriated $3,000 for the requisition and preservation of a herd of Texas Longhorns. Unlike the buffalo, the Texas Longhorn did not vanish from an astounding slaughter, but was almost cross-bred away.

Scientists are re-discovering the Longhorns as a genetic goldmine for an ailing cattle industry.

"It will be a relief for health-conscious consumers to learn that compared with other breeds and cross breeds, the Longhorns and Longhorn cross breeds produced a high quality, lean carcass that surpassed the Hereford with less outside trim fat, more desirable grades, less muscle fat, and more unsaturated fats. The relatively high percentage of unsaturated fatty acids found in Longhorn beef is a story of significance that needs to be told . . ." [1]

"In 1984, tests conducted by Chicago and Gainesville, Florida, laboratories on a surplus bull from Longhorn Lean, Inc. revealed a cholesterol content of less than half that of chicken, equal to flounder." [2]

1. Dr. Steward H. Fowler, " 'Beefing-Up' Consumer Demand with Texas Longhorn Genes," *Texas Longhorn Journal,* January 1989.
2. "Hellenbeck's WR Longhorns," *Texas Longhorn Journal,* January 1989.

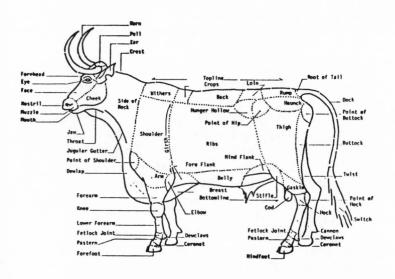

CATTLE TRAILS

early towns that faded as train service diverted traffic. The church is chief remaining structure. George West's principal industries are uranium mining and ranching. The Nueces River Bottom in the Coastal Bend was the original stronghold where Texas Longhorn trail drives originated.

Geronimo — Famous Longhorn steer that resides in a glass-sided case on the Courthouse square. Geronimo was owned by Mr. George West and was one of his most valued "Sanchos" or lead steers for the cattle drives north. After leading herds north for many years, Geronimo was allowed to live out his last years on the West ranch and when he died, he was mounted. Mr. West never liked the original taxidermy job, so in 1970, Geronimo was redone and a new climate controlled cage was built. Before he came home, however, he made a tour of Russia as part of a Cultural Exchange Project.

Armontrout Museum — U.S. 181 at the south edge of the city. Antique-filled home that provides local and pioneer history. Cactus garden and picnic area nearby. Admission.

Live Oak County Museum — County Courthouse — Mon.–Fri. 8–5 P.M. Historical relics and documents of early Live Oak County.

GOLIAD

Located at the crossroads of Hwys. 59 and 77A/183, Goliad is the gateway to Mexico or the beaches of the Gulf Coast from the northeast. It is the third oldest municipality in the state and a place forever remembered in the pages of Texas history. The town was first named Santa Doretea by the Spaniards in the 16th century and then named La Bahia when the Presidio and Mission Espiritu de Zuniga were moved there in 1749. In 1829, the name Goliad was officially adopted. Goliad was the smallest town in Texas to be selected for the Main Street Program 1984 and the Courthouse Square Historic District is one of the most complete examples of early Texas settlements.

Camping — nearby Coleto Creek.

Points of Interest: La Bahia Downs — located on U.S. 183 north of Goliad, features quarter horse races at various times during the year.

Goliad State Historical Park — Located approximately one-quarter mile south of Goliad, Texas, on U.S. Highway 183. It contains 178 acres of gently rolling terrain. The Texas Parks and Wildlife Department maintains the unit of the park that is open all year with facilities for picnicking, hiking, tent and trailer camping, and both historic and nature study. The campsites range from primitive to those with water, sewer, and electrical connections. Screened shelters with electricity, water, tables and cooking grills are available.

Nature Trails — The trail heads from the mission buildings and picnic grounds and traverses typical South Texas brushland or chaparral. The brushland contrasts sharply with the luxuriant gallery woodlands of the San Antonio River floodplain. Bird life along the trail is especially varied due to diverse habitat and to mild regional climate.

Honeycomb Antiques — on the town square.

Goliad County Courthouse — along with the 19th and early 20th century structures surrounding it, was listed in the National Register of Historic Places in 1976. The Second Empire style courthouse, designated by noted Texas architect Alfred Giles, was completed in 1894. Limestone used in the construction was hauled from Austin by oxcart. Restored and enlarged in 1964, the courthouse is a Recorded Texas Historic Landmark.

St. Stephen's Episcopal Church — Began as a mission in 1861. Church building was erected in 1881 and elevated to Parish in 1913. This is only one of the fine examples of early structures which are still in use in Goliad today.

49

The Goliad Flag — Raised following the Texas Declaration of Independence, December 20, 1835. The severed arm and bloody sword signified that Texians would rather lose an arm than remain under the yoke of a tyrant.

Presidio La Bahia — The oldest fort in the Western United States and the only Texas Revolution site with its original 1836 appearance. There have been 9 flags flown over the Presidio and it is the location of the longest siege in American military history. The saddest page of Texas history occurred here, the Goliad Massacre. This represents the largest single loss of life in the cause of Texas Independence and inspired the battle cry "remember Goliad" at the battle of San Jacinto.

Mission Espiritu Santo — Mission Espiritu Santo was founded in 1722 near Matagorda Bay to serve the Karankawa Indians. In 1749, the mission was relocated on the north bank of the San Antonio River. In the mid 18th century, the Franciscan Order

and Indian converts operated a large cattle ranch and the buildings were used for educational purposes from 1847 to 1862. It is located in the Goliad State Park and is open for visitors. The exquisite frescoes have been preserved and restored.

Grave of Col. Fannin and Troops — On Palm Sunday, March 27, 1836, the men were led out in three directions from La Bahia and massacred; the wounded were shot in the compound of the Fort. The bodies were stripped and left unburied. General Thomas Rusk and army gathered the remains and gave them a complete military funeral on Friday, June 3, 1836.

Fannin Plaza — Corner of Market and Franklin Streets. A place where visitors may enjoy a picnic lunch or just sit and take themselves back in time. Texas Revolution cannons and memorial statue to Col. Fannin and men were erected in April 1885.

Goliad — General Ignacio Zaragoza
— Photo by Richard Siemens

Goliad — Mission Espiritu Santo
— Photo by Richard Siemens

51

Hanging Tree (Cart War Oak) — located on Courthouse lawn. Court was held under this tree during the 1857 Cart War and the guilty were promptly hanged.

Getzwiller Home — located on Market St. A cornerstone dates the building as built in 1853.

Blacksmith Shop — 301 E. Fannin. Built in the 1890s and still in use. Cattle brands are burned on doors and windows.

Masonic Temple — Corner S. Commercial and Franklin Sts. Constructed and dedicated in 1854. Goliad Lodge No. 94.

Baptist Oak Tree — 200 S. Chilton. A bronze plaque states that under this tree the First Baptist Church of Goliad was organized in May of 1849.

Market House Museum — Corner of S. Market and Franklin Sts. Official Historical Medallion. Designated a State Archaeological Landmark in May of 1981. Built by the city in the early 1870s and contained stalls which were rented to farmers for the sale of meat and produce. Firehouse hook and ladder was added in the 1880s. It is now a museum and the office of the Goliad County Chamber of Commerce.

Mission San Rosario — (Now in ruins) — Historical marker located 4 miles west on Highway 59. Founded in November 1754, for the Karankawa Indians.

Fannin Battleground — Nine miles east of Goliad on Hwy. 59 is the site of the Battle of Coleto Creek. In March 1836, during the Texas Revolution, Texas troops under Col. Fannin surrendered to superior Mexican forces.

Goliad Auditorium — A Texas Centennial structure dedicated in 1937. On the left front facade, three stone panels tell the story of Goliad. Also located on this facade are five friezes showing the names of Texas heroes. These friezes are separated with medallions of the five-pointed Texas star. At the main entrance, the medallions depict a pioneer man and woman, an Indian, a Padre, a longhorn, and a large shield telling the story of Goliad.

Annual Events: Christmas in Goliad — Celebration blends cultural traditions of more than a century ago. Sat.: Festivities on historic courthouse square include holiday entertainment, handmade arts & crafts, antique toy show, gun and knife exhibit, homes tour, bingo, and holiday foods with reindeer burgers and old-fashioned candy store. (512) 645-3115 or 645-3563.

Texas Frontier Rendez-vous — December — Texas Brigade of Skinners encamp at Presidio La Bahia, demonstrating everyday lifestyles of pre-1840s Texians. Traders row, arts & crafts, tomahawk and knife-throwing contests. (512) 645-3752.

Fiesta of Our Lady of Lorets — December — Celebration at Presidio La Bahia honoring feast day of the patroness of the fort chapel. Evening Mass followed by refreshments and holiday festivities. (512) 645-3752.

Feast of Our Lady of Guadalupe — Celebration in Goliad State Park honors legendary appearance of the Mother of God to the humble Indian Juan Diego in Mexico in 1531. Luminarios line walls, walkways and interior of restored Mission Espiritu Santo for the sacred event. Virgin of Guadalupe Mass in the evening includes traditional Spanish songs composed by original missionaries. (512) 645-3405.

U.S. Air Force Band of the West Concert — February — Evening performance in city's auditorium. (512) 645-2666.

Goliad County Fair and Rodeo — March — fairgrounds, carnival, foods, show animals, parade, chili cookoff, Go Texas & Children's Activities. (512) 645-3563.

Fannin Memorial Service — March — only living history event of its kind in the states; historical re-enactment honors the largest sacrifice of life for Texas Independence when Col. James W. Fannin and his men were massacred at Goliad March 27, 1836. (512) 645-3563.

Longhorn Stampede — June — Foods and entertainment on county fairgrounds. Gun fights, arts & crafts, chili cookoff, auction, volleyball tourney, dance. (512) 645-3563.

Galvez Fiesta & Spanish Nightwatch — June — Living history program celebrating the La Bahia connection with the American Revolution. (512) 645-3752.

La Bahia Downs — Horse Races — (512) 645-8208.

Capture of Goliad — October — Pays homage to anniversary of a time in the struggle for Texas independence. Living history program at Presidio La Bahia. (512) 645-3752.

Magee-Gutierrez Expedition — November — Expedition Living History Program at Presidio La Bahia. (512) 645-3752.

INDIANOLA

From Port Lavaca, take Texas 238 (Austin St.) approximately two miles to where it goes right at a fork with Texas 316; continuing straight puts you on 316; go a little over eight miles to beach.

The only man left standing in town is La Salle, or rather a monument to him. He is the French explorer who landed here in 1685 and was later murdered at the hands of his own men. At one time, Indianola was one of the busiest ports on the Gulf of Mexico and the main port of entry for new colonists arriving in Texas. Several distinguished men came through Indianola. Jefferson Davis, as U.S. Secretary of War, shipped Arabian camels here as an experiment to replace army horses in the western desert. Prince Carl zu Solms-Braunfels, who founded New Braunfels and Fredericksburg, arrived here from Germany. Indianola withstood the Civil War, including Union shellings, yellow fever epidemics, and two hurricanes (1866 and 1875). Those two killed more than 900 people. In 1886 a hurricane completely washed two towns away. It is sad that a town that withstood so much finally succumbed to a hurricane. It didn't die without a fight, however.

Very old, interesting cemetery here.

Indianola — Catch of the day

U.S.S. WISCONSIN

U.S.S. LEXINGTON

INGLESIDE

Ingleside was once known as "Palomas" meaning "doves." In 1830 colonists came through Aransas Pass, a narrow inlet, between St. Joseph's and Mustang Islands, and landed at McGloin's Bluff, on Copano Bay, between where Ingleside is now located and Harbor Island — now known as "the Humble Docks." In 1850 a ranch was built on the bay in the cove area, by Marcellus and George Turner, and was called "Ingleside" from a poem of Robert Burns, in which he refers to the fireside as "Ingleside." Thus the post received the same name, and so did all the settlements that grew up around it. At one time it was a thriving city with fine motels and marinas. Future growth is imminent with Home Port headed their way.

Points of Interest: Oak Park — 90 acre park off of Sherry Avenue.

Ingleside Museum — Tuesday 1–4; Sat. 9–4. Located on Highway 1069 and 361. Fresh seafood can be found at locations around Ingleside Cove.

Annual Events: Ingleside Round-up Days — May — (512) 776-2906.

KENEDY

One of the most historically colorful towns in the entire Coastal Bend is Kenedy. It may be said that it has more past than present. In the days of its youth, it was known as "Six Shooter Junction," and the name was well earned. The rich river bottom land first supported a village of Lipan Apaches. They were joined in 1735 by Spanish soldiers. Captain Mifflin

Ingleside — Speckled Trout

Kenedy — ever present windmill

Kenedy, a partner of Richard King, of King Ranch, purchased land for a townsite here in 1886. It was on the Chisholm Trail over which great herds of Longhorn steers were
trailed to market in Kansas. It was an important stagecoach
stop that became infested with bandits and rustlers who came
to prey on stagecoach passengers and freighters and to steal
cattle and horses. It was in this vicinity that John Wesley Har-
din began his infamous reputation as a gunman and killer.
These outlaws originated a bloody form of personal encounter
known as the Helena Duel. It consisted of tying the left hands
of the duelists together with rawhide, giving each a knife with
a three-inch blade, whirling them around rapidly a few times
and turning them loose. The shortness of the knife blades pre-
vented a single fatal stroke and the fight became a gory slash-
ing match with the contestants hacking away furiously. No
quarter was given or expected. Only after the Karnes County
vigilance committee and the Texas Rangers began to apply
their six-gun justice was the area cleared of the "gentry of the
brush." Many "fightin' and feudin' " families are written
about and their stories may be read about in the local libraries

and Chamber of Commerce. Today Kenedy is a quiet community full of friendly folks.

Boating and fishing — Six major lakes are within easy driving distance of Kenedy. The Gulf of Mexico is 90 miles south.

Hunting — dove, quail, javelina, ducks, geese, turkey and deer provide ample opportunities.

ᴜᴜ H.C. ੪ ᴄℬ S

PANNA MARIA

This is the oldest permanent Polish settlement in America. Their first midnight mass was celebrated in 1854 under the old oak tree which still stands at the site of the present Panna Maria Catholic Church.

Ruckman House 1878 — The Karnes County Historical Society is actively involved in preserving many local historic sites.

Seraphic Sisters Home — diverse architectural styles, ranging from simply functional to lavishly ornate, give Panna Maria an unusual appeal. Many older homes are undergoing restoration.

Annual Events: Bluebonnet Days — Music, arts & crafts, snake handling, parade, carnival and other family fun fill the weekend of the annual spring festival named for the colorful state flower which blooms in abundance along area highways and fields.

Christmas in Kenedy — December — Arts & Crafts Show in Civic Center. (512) 583-3223.

KINGSVILLE

This unique town is located about 40 miles southwest of Corpus Christi between the Rio Grande and Nueces Rivers. At one time, the area was scorned by an ill-informed Congress as a desert wasteland, a place no one would want. In the early 1800s, Spanish ranches operated along the Santa Gertrudis and Los Olmos creeks. Trouble with the Indians caused the ranchers to abandon their claims and leave their homes to roam the sparse terrain. "Wild Horse Desert" was the name given the area by the time Capt. Richard King purchased an old Spanish land grant on the Santa Gertrudis Creek. He was a former ship captain who founded the world famous King Ranch, and the city of Kingsville is his namesake. His son-in-law, Robert J. Kleberg, sought northern capital to build the St. Louis, Brownsville, and Mexican Railroad from Corpus Christi to Brownsville. Today it is the home of Texas A&I University, industrial plants, and headquarters of King Ranch. Its economy is based on petro-chemical, agricultural, and ranching operations.

Points of Interest: Historic Cattle Dipping Vat — On Highway 77 in Kingsville, near Missouri-Pacific RR and Caesar Pens. In 1894 this vat — believed to be the first in the world — was built to stop the spread of tick fever, which was destroying thousands of U.S. beef cattle. The mortality rate from tick fever sometimes reached 90%. Thankfully longhorns and other native southwestern cattle were immune. They did, however, carry the insect, which could infect other animals. Officials from Texas A&M College and the U.S. Bureau of Animal Industry headed the efforts to eradicate the tick (Margaropus annulatus). Manager of the King Ranch, R. J. Kleberg, allowed the vat to be built, and 25,000 tick-infested cattle from the ranch were dipped. An effective formula of oil and sulphur was discovered here. In October 1898, the U.S. quarantine was lifted for cattle, thanks to treatment received in the dip.

We'd be remiss if we didn't print this famous recipe for what just might be the best-loved recipe in Texas. Nobody really knows how the dish earned its name, or its connection to the illustrious ranch.

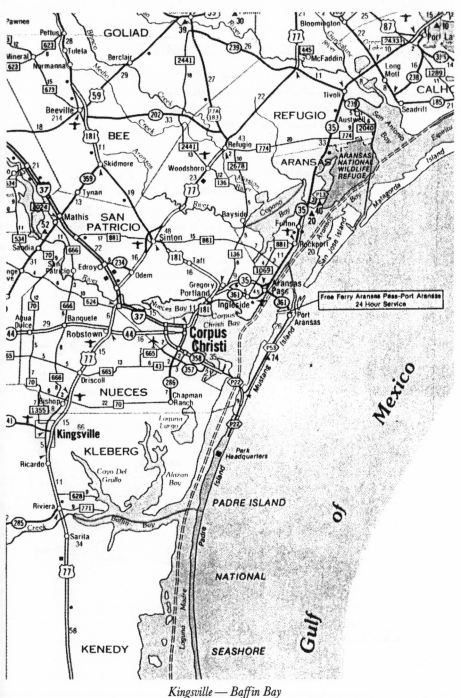

Kingsville — Baffin Bay

KING RANCH CHICKEN CASSEROLE

1 3-lb. chicken, boiled, boned, cubed
1 pkg. tortillas, cut in 1-inch strips
1¹/₂ cups grated cheddar cheese
1 large onion, chopped
1 can cream of mushroom soup
1 can cream of chicken soup
1¹/₂ cup chicken broth (from cooking chicken)
1 10-oz. can Ro-Tel Tomatoes & Green Chiles

Combine broth, soups, and tomatoes and set aside. In a large oiled casserole dish layer half of tortilla pieces, half of chicken, half of onion and half of cheese. Pour half of liquid mixture over layers. Repeat layers of tortillas, chicken, and onion, then pour remaining liquid mixture over. Top with remaining cheese. Bake at 375 degrees for 1 hour. This is even better when reheated!

John Conner Museum — Texas A&I University, 820 Santa Gertrudis. (512) 595-2819. Monday through Friday 10–5, Sunday 2:30–5. Free. This museum as well as the South Texas Archives preserve the history of this area noted for its variety. Lifelike dioramas, slide shows, lectures, touch and feel areas, Indian, Spanish, and Texas pioneer relics, combine to make this museum well worth your while. The area ethnic culture and archeology are emphasized with guns, swords, and fossils.

King Ranch — Texas Hwy. 141 west 2.5 miles (512) 592-6411. Open seven days 8–4. Pick up a map or rent a guide-cassette at the gatehouse. The drive includes views of feeding pens, show pens, and pastures containing cattle and quarter horses. Deer are often present on the loop road. Steamboat Captain Richard King's philosophy was rather simple: Buy land and never sell. That is just what he did. The ranch was founded in 1867, when he purchased the 75,000-acre Santa Gertrudis spread. It was originally a Spanish land grant. By 1961 King, in partnership with Mifflin Kenedy and James Walworth, had 20,000 cattle and 3,000 horses. Today it is the largest in the United States, consisting of 825,000 acres. Its original claim to fame arose with the development of the famous Santa Gertrudis breed, the first cattle strain developed by man in the Western Hemisphere. Today the ranch has become a diversified enterprise with interest in several foreign countries. In the 1940s, it began breeding racehorses. Two King Ranch thoroughbreds have won the Kentucky Derby.

Dick Kleberg Park — South edge of city on Loop 428. (512) 592-5229. Open seven days a week, dawn to dusk. Free. Picnic tables, grills, lake, fishing pier, Navy jet fighter for the kids to climb on. There are 211 shaded creek-side acres.

Kleberg County Recreation Park — Hwy 77 bypass one mile, turn left onto Military Hwy. one quarter of a mile southeast of city limits. (512) 592-1101. Open seven days a week from 7:30–11. Free. 18-hole golf course ($4 greens fee) and tennis courts.

Leo Kauffer Park — Take US. Hwy 77 south nine miles, turn left onto FM Rd. 628 and go east 14 miles. About 23 miles from town. (512) 297-5738. Open seven days a week 8–9. Park offers saltwater recreation areas on the upper reaches of Baffin Bay, which opens into the Laguna Madre inside Padre Island National Seashore. Camping $2 per night, hookups, $4 per night.

Seller's Market — 205 E. Kleberg — (512) 595-4992. This rustic little center features handmade treasures, home-baked goods, crafts, paintings, jewelry, workshops, demonstrations and tea room. For a fee, members may join & sell items on commission. Restaurant is open Wed.–Fri., for lunch. The menu varies daily and is generally interesting and good.

Annual Events: Annual Children's Show — (512) 595-3901.

Texas A&I Rodeo — March — First weekend — J. K. Northway Exposition Center — (512) 595-3713.

Kleberg County Fair — March — J. K. Northway Exposition Center — (512) 574-5229.

Kleberg County Youth Rodeo — July — (512) 592-6438.

Texas A&I Jazz Festival — March — Held at Jones Auditorium on Texas A&I campus; competitions, evening concert featuring university jazz band and guest band. (512) 595-2803.

Coastal Bend Regional History Fair — March — (512) 595-2810.

Annual George Strait Team Roping Competition — June — George Strait concert on Sat.; J. K. Northway Exposition Center. (512) 592-8516.

Juneteenth Celebration — (512) 592-6438.

Miller Blastoff Fireworks — July — (512) 573-2401.

Hispanic Heritage Week Celebration — (512) 592-6438.

Spring Festival — April — a two-week celebration on Texas A&I University campus. Events include Blue Angel Air Show at Kingsville Naval Air Station, Fashion Show & Dinner, Arts & Crafts Show, Automobile, Boats,  & Farm Equipment Show, Parade, Golf Tourney, Battle of Country/Western Bands, UIL One-Act Plays, Taste of Kleberg Co., Student Carnival, Area Tour of J. E. Conner Museum, Horse Center, Henrietta Memorial Museum, Seller's Market, Naval Air Station, King Ranch, Int'l. Style Show, Int'l. Student Bazaar (food tasting event), South Texas Pinto Bean Cookoff, Ballet Folklorico, Battle of Hispanic Bands & Dance, Spring Formal Dance, Battle of Popular Bands & Dance, Festival of Christian Music (Churches from all areas invited to participate), Quilt Show, Pickle & Cake Contests, Evening AG Roundup Barbeque, UIL Student Competition, Wild Game Feast, and a Parachute Show. Whew! (512) 585-3986.

Fourth of July Community Celebration and Fireworks Display — (512) 592-6438.

Fiesta De Colores Art Festival — October — (512) 584-2196.

Carnivale — October — (512) 592-6438.

Celebrity Auction — November — (512) 592-6438.

King Ranch Bull and Quarter Horse Sale and BBQ.

Christmas Parade and Tree Lighting Ceremony (512) 592-8516.

Christmas Tree Forest.

A week in O' Bethlehem — December — Week-long Christmas pageant hosted by 23 area churches and other organizations; in J. K. Northway Exposition Center. Guides escort visitors through old-time Marketplace where crafters in authentic costume demonstrate 2,000-year-old crafts and skills. Tent City with tax collector, prophets and ancient storytellers; Hebrew wedding party where visitors can dance the Hora. Also, live nativity scene, music from the time of Christ, arts & crafts, foods, and much more. (512) 592-8818.

Martin Luther King, Jr. Day Parade — (512) 592-8516.

Music Club Competition — Texas A&I Music Hall — students from throughout the world compete; concert by noted performer, accompanied by Texas A&I Symphonic Band, workshops, finals. (512) 592-2374.

LAMAR — See Rockport

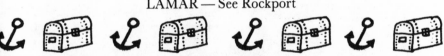

MATHIS

This community was founded in 1889 by Thomas Henry Mathis. Farming and ranching are still prevalent.

Lake Corpus Christi — one of the largest fresh water lakes in Texas. Provides trailer parks, campgrounds, historical points of interest around the lake such as Echo Stagecoach Depot, Ghost

Town, Lagarto (1856), old San Patricio (1830), Fort Lipaniland, Fort Casa Blanca, and Dinero (named for gold buried there by Santa Anna's fleeing soldiers after defeat at San

Lamar — Schoenstatt Convent
— Photo by Richard Siemens

Lamar — The Big Tree (famous liveoak)
— Photo by Richard Siemens

Mathis — goin' fishin'

Jacinto). A few miles west of Dinero is the home where J. Frank Dobie, noted Texas author, was born and raised.

NORMANNA

The settlement that originated near here is not Normanna. It dates from about 1850. The first town in the area, two miles west of present day Normanna, was called San Domingo for its location near the junction of San Domingo and Dry Medio creeks. After the railroad was built in 1886, its citizens moved to Walton, a new flag station on the rail line. The name "Walton" honored the town's sheriff, D. A. T. Walton. When Norwegians settled the area in the 1890s, Walton became Normanna. The word originally suggested the qualities of old Norse heroes, but through local usage came to mean "Home of the Norseman." The town thrived for years,

Normanna — cactus in bloom

then declined after a series of fires and the advent of the automobile.

Normanna Days — pioneer celebration held annually.

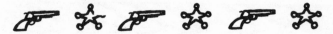

OAKVILLE

On Hwy. 37 — 12 miles north of the junction of Hwy. 59 and 37. The town has a historic old jail and city hall. The townsite was designated in 1856, and was at one time the county seat of Live Oak County. The creek nearby is supposedly the last place a person was hanged from a tree in Texas. Oldtimers will be glad to sit a spell and relate factual stories about early Oakville which are amazing but true. Lynching, horsestealing, Indian uprisings, it all happened in little bitty old Oakville.

Van's — The epitome of a "real" Texas Bar-be-Que establishment. The moment you walk in the door you are in for a treat at Van's. The food is good, served on butcher paper. A

68

Oakville

Odem — jackrabbit

— Photo by Richard Siemens

69

player piano bawls out rinky tink tunes for a quarter while you enjoy your meal. Texas memorabilia is on every wall, such as barbed wire (pronounced Bob War down here), photographs of recent trail riders to San Antonio, and arrowhead displays.

ODEM

Odem lies on flat grassy coastal plains varied by a little brush country in the west. Founded in 1909.

The Silver Lining — features old world charm of antiques, quilts, country crafts, collectibles. (512) 368-2124.

Junk and Jewels — classic example of a junk collector's paradise. Some antiques. Closed Thursdays and Sundays. 705 Voss. (512) 368-2066.

PADRE ISLAND

Padre Island allows its visitors to get away from it all without going far. This island, partially located within the city limits of Corpus Christi and only 30 minutes from downtown or the airport, is a perfect vacation spot. It is a barrier island stretching 110 miles along the Gulf Coast and offers year-round fun in the sun. Padre Island has a colorful history. Small Indian tribes once hunted and fished here. Shipwrecks, hurricanes, cattle ranches, and oil and gas exploration have all added their artifacts to its tale.

In 1519, Alfonso Alvarez de Pineda discovered and charted the island on behalf of Governor Garay of Jamaica. First named Las Islas Blancas — the White Island — the long island became infamous as a graveyard for ships driven onto this shore by storms out of the Gulf of Mexico. The most famous shipwreck occurred in 1553, when a 20-ship Spanish treasure fleet ran into a hurricane. Many of the galleons broke up on the island. Of some 300 survivors of the storm, only two

survived the fierce Karankawa Indian attacks and hardships of the march down the coast to Mexico.

Later the Island got its present name from Padre Jose Nicolas Balli, whose family had migrated from Spain in 1569. They became wealthy landowners in the Rio Grande Valley and were influential in military and government affairs. Padre Balli was ordained in 1790 and applied to Spain's King Charles IV in 1880 for 11.5 leagues of land on the island. Balli began the first settlement on the island in 1804. It was named Rancho Santa Cruz and was located about 26 miles from the southern tip of the island. Balli's first task was to Christianize the Karankawa Indians. With the help of his nephew, Padre Balli started his own ranch and brought in herds of cattle, sheep and horses.*

Points of Interest: Seagull Park — city park away from the water. Approximately 6 acres located on Jackfish Drive    (down the street from Whataburger). Covered picnic tables, wooden playground structure, baseball backstop, and jogging path open to the public.

Bob Hall Pier — open 24 hours to the public as a fishing pier with admission charge of 50 cents per person. Rod, reel, and bait rentals and purchases are available. Cost is $1.00. Must use your own equipment on the pier. Pier extends beyond the third sand bar into Gulf of Mexico.

---

* Vernon Smylie, *This is Padre Island*, Texas News Syndicate Press, 1964.

J. P. Luby Surf Park —
Nueces County Park with surfing pier made especially for the
sport. The surfing pier is designed to increase wave action.
Festivities are held at this location on the Gulf of Mexico
during spring break and on many holiday weekends. Surfboards may be rented along the seawall and at many island
shops.

Padre Island National Seashore — created
by the Department of the Interior in September
1962, the 134,000-acre coastline area is reserved
for public recreation. RV sites, information office, and artifact displays are included in the facilities. The entrance to Padre Island National Seashore is
near the southern end of Park Road 22. One can drive a con-
ventional car 14 miles south from the northern entrance. Further travel requires a 4-wheel drive vehicle as the sands are
soft, intermixed with tiny shells, and will not support an ordi-
nary passenger car. Malaquite Beach is one of the few areas
where driving is prohibited. Driving is allowed, however, on
the majority of Padre Island beaches.

Big Shell and Little Shell Beaches —
famous spots located inside the national
seashore for great shelling and less crowded
areas. 4-wheel drive vehicles are a must 12
miles south on the beach, noted by a large
sign. Check with hotels/condos for 4-wheel
drive rentals.

C-Sculpture — Sand sculptors have a fantastic opportunity to release their creative urges and win prizes. Spectators
will delight in the sights at the J. P. Luby Youth Park on
Padre Island. Teams of participants compete to create the
largest, most elaborate and original entries, beginning as early
as dawn. For registration information call sponsor KNCN at
(512) 289-1000. Day-long entertainment, free.

Grasslands Nature Trail — Just inside the national seashore boundary. Native plants are designated in this 2-mile
asphalt walk among wildflowers. Overlooks provided for com-

72

Padre Island National Seashore

mon animal life.

Safety Advice: While the beach is great, it can also be dangerous. Several safety tips are advised to help individuals avoid hazards.

Broken glass — Wear shoes even when wading to insure that you don't get cut by broken glass or sharp shells.

Portuguese man-of-war jellyfish — The sting of these creatures is quite painful. Some persons can be dangerously allergic to their sting. Sometimes the pain is relieved by meat tenderizer. Carry a bottle of tenderizer in your glove compartment when going to the beach. Often the man-of-war can be seen floating on the water, but not always. There are many varieties of jellyfish. This variety is one of the more common in this area.

Rattlesnakes — In this area, snakes are present throughout the year. Be particularly mindful walking in grassy, brushy areas and at night. Do not reach into hand-sized burrows in the dunes.

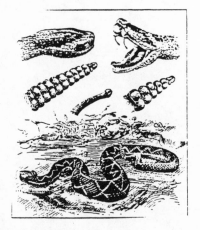

Stingrays and sharks — Occasionally come close to shore. Incidents with stingrays are more numerous than with sharks. Shark attacks, though rare, have occurred in this area. Stingrays have a barb on their tail that lances into the body. The barb also has a poison that is extremely painful.

Swimming — Never swim alone or away from others. Watch out for undertows. Keep a close watch on small children in the surf. Few beaches have lifeguards.

Cars — Although there are legal and practical limits to

speed on the beach, look both ways before crossing car ruts to be safe.

Car stuck in sand — Note the tide and do not park your vehicle where the rising tide can engulf it. Always carry a shovel and car jack to help you dig out if necessary.

Sunburn — Overexposure to the sun can make for a miserable few days that are easily avoided. Be discreet about the amount of time you are in direct sunlight and use sunblock and hats.

PAWNEE

A homesick lad from Pawnee inadvertently gave the community its name. He was a Kansas immigrant approaching manhood. One night, when he was sitting around the campfire, most probably contemplating home and loved ones, he picked up a piece of soft pine and, heating a wire from the coals of the fire, burned the name "Pawnee" into the pine. Later, he posted the board by nailing it to a nearby tree. The name stuck for the community.

PETTUS

 This small town was settled in the 1850s when John Freeman Pettus (1808–1878) set up his sprawling ranch about four miles south of here. Pettus is the oil capital of Bee County. John Pettus, the son of one of Stephen F. Austin's first 300 colonists, was an extensive cattle and horse breeder. Earlier the town had been called "Dry Medio" for a nearby creek. It was named after John Pettus during the Civil War. In 1886, the sleepy town awoke to become the cattle shipping center for the area, when the San Antonio and Aransas Pass Railroad ran a

Pawnee — wildflowers

Pettus — oil rig

line through the area.

First Christian Church — The corner of Walton and Commerce Streets. Pettus. Built in 1905, this edifice is the first church to serve the needs of the Protestants in Pettus. The church was called a Christian Church at the request of a land donor, Mrs. S. B. Hodges. Contributions for its construction came from all denominations. On August 29, 1906, the First Christian Church (Disciples of Christ) was organized with 25 members. For many years Baptists, Methodists, and Disciples conducted a union Sunday School and worshipped here. Its tall, white spire became the town landmark.

PORT ARANSAS

Balmy Gulf breezes, sunshine, and the roar of the surf are waiting for you in Port Aransas, affectionately called "Port A" by local yokels. If you are looking for the bright lights and glamour of the big city, you're in the wrong spot. But you're in the right spot if you're looking for relaxation, fishing, leisurely cruises, duck hunting, sailing, and a host of other activities.

Points of Interest: The Fudge Factory — located inside the Port A Beach Company, Alister Street, this unique little factory gives new meaning to the word fudge. If you think you've heard an assortment of fudge flavors, try these on for size: Cookies 'n Creme, Banana Pudding, Banana Split, Vanilla, Vanilla Walnut, Maple Walnut, Caramel, Caramel Pecan, Caramel Butterscotch, Strawberry, Peanut Butter, Chocolate Sprinkle, S'mores, Mint Chocolate Swirl, Rocky Road Pecan, Chewy Praline, and the much in demand favorite, Jalapeno Fudge! Stop in for a free sample and you won't be able to resist more.

The Lighthouse — One of the oldest landmarks. For al-

Port Aransas — lighthouse in Liggett Channel
— Photo by Richard Siemens

most 90 years its light was a reassuring sign for mariners seeking the channel entrance. It was built on the flats of Lydia Ann Island. The lens is 67 feet above the marshy land and came from France. It was hand polished a century ago. The Lighthouse has scars from the Civil War. One version is that the Confederate soldiers took the lens down and buried it to prevent Yankee Block-aders from operating it, should it be captured. The Confederate soldiers attempted to blow up the tower with dynamite to keep the Union armies from taking over. They did not destroy the tower but damage was done to the extent that it had to be rebuilt in 1867. The brick walls at the base are approximately 4 feet thick. The interior has 69 wedge-shaped steps that circle up to the light. The original source of light was a kerosene lamp. Later the lamp was replaced by a 500-watt electric light.

Tarpon Inn — Built in 1886 — Vintage wooden structure that is still popular though unrestored. Has housed some V.I.P.s such as Franklin D. Roosevelt and Duncan Hines, who spent his honeymoon there. Seafood restaurant; 26 rooms with baths.

University of Texas Marine Science Institute — Along the ship channel between Mustang and San Jose Island. Open weekdays. Laboratory and research facility. Displays include Gulf marine life, plants, and fascinating introduction to oceanography. Seven aquariums show sealife from the marshy wetlands to the floor of the ocean. Shell display. Films are available for showing tour groups upon request. Take Cotter Street and go east, turn left into the parking lot just before you get to the beach. If you get to the beach you've gone too far. Open 8–5 weekdays. (512) 749-6729.

Fishing on your own: Horace Caldwell Pier — on the beach at the end of Beach Street. Concession, bait, fee per person and per rod.

J. P. Luby Pier — at Roberts Point Park across from the Dennis Dreyer Municipal Marina. Free; no amenities other than restroom facilities at the harbormaster's office.

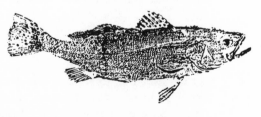

Ancel Brundrett Pier — at the north end of Station Street. Cast out into the Corpus Ship Channel for redfish, trout, mackerel, sheepshead. Free. Restrooms.

Nueces County Pier — at the unpaved end of Port Street on a spot of land locally referred to as "Charlie's Pasture." Fish the ship channel for red, flounder, trout, drum, or take a crab net for blue crab and rock crab. Free; no amenities.

Surf fishing — presents itself on all of Mustang Island where it does not interfere with swimmers. Don't forget that

Beach Parking Permits ($5 per year) are necessary in most of the three miles of city beach. Funds from the permits are earmarked specifically for daily cleaning of the beach, and building and maintaining the portable restrooms on the beach.

Sail Club — on Alister Street between the Super S and Ice Box. Live music most weekends alternates between country and rock. Play pool or darts.

San Jose Island — across the Corpus Christi Ship Channel from Port Aransas. This is a privately owned island but the beaches are public. Accessible only by boat. The Jetty Boat ferries passengers daily, 6:30 A.M. and 7 A.M., then hourly until noon and again at 2, 4, and 6 P.M. Buy tickets and board at Woody's Boat Basin, (512) 749-5271. $7 for adults and $4 for children age 10 and under. Bring sunscreen, food, drinks, bikes, dogs, cats, kids, and fishing poles but no motorized vehicles. You're on your own, there are no amenities on San Jose. Beachcomb, swim, sun, fish, jog, and bike.

U.S. Coast Guard Station — 800 N. Station. (512) 749-5217. Reserve one day in advance, groups over 15 must give two days' notice. Free.

Tours conducted Tuesday through Thursday and weekends from 10 to 4. Includes 30–45 minute narrated tour of station, smaller rescue boats as well as the *Point Baker,* an 82-foot vessel.

Fishing Charters — the slogan in this town is, "Here, they bite every day. You just have to go fishin' to catch 'em!" President Roosevelt's trophies used to be displayed at the Tarpon Inn.

Deep Sea Headquarters — 416 W. Cotter, (512) 749-5597. Two party boats with concessions for group fishing, private charters for one to six anglers. Most offshore fishing trips are made for eight hours. Shorter trips available if demand warrants them. Reserve private charters in

advance. Tackle and bait provided. Bring your food and drink on private charters.

Port Aransas — sea oats in sand dunes

Port Aransas — shell gathering

Fisherman's Wharf — 1 Tarpon, (512) 749-5448. Two party boats take anglers snapper and kingfishing for four, six, eight, and 12 hour trips. Private charters accommodate one to six people with bait, ice and tackle provided. Bring your own food and drink. Gulf and backbay charters available. Reserve in advance.

Diablo — (512) 749-4598, Box 86, Port Aransas, Texas 78373, April–October is 8 hours dock to dock off-shore fishing for kingfish, dorado, ling, mackerel, bonito, black fin tuna and shark. Everything provided except your food and drink. Ice chest on board for your use. Advance reservations, $100 deposit required.

Dolphin Docks, 404 W. Cotter, (512) 749-6624. Fishing for one to 100 for private or company charters. Fish the gulf for shark or red snapper and more, or head for the bays for redfish, black drum, flounder and trout. Bait, ice and tackle provided. Ask about food and drink availability. Reserve in advance.

Island Moorings Marina — Park Road 53 next to airport, (512) 749-4983. Private charters for two to six for half and full day excursions. By appointment 24 hours in advance. Bait, tackle, ice, food and drink provided for gulf or bay charters.

Woody's — 114 Cotter, (512) 749-5271. Charters for one to six people for bay or gulf fishing. Fish from 7 A.M. to 3 P.M. Bait, tackle, ice provided; you bring food and drink. Reserve in advance.

Scuba Diving Charters — Dolphin Docks, 404 W. Cotter, (512) 749-6624. The Sharkhunter Express takes certified divers out for eight hours of diving with a divemaster. Bring your own equipment and proof of certification. Excursions depend on the weather and water temperature. Reserve in advance.

"Rig Fishin' ": One of the most popular sports around. Beg, borrow, rent, or steal a boat and go! Cruise to off-shore. Fishing around the rigs is superb. Trolling, diving, and spearfishing is always fun, sometimes outstanding! Ling, snapper, redfish, barracuda, mackerel, bonita, kingfish, shark, grouper, and gulf trout are just a few of the possibilities!

Seafood Markets: Bandit Seafood (512) 749-7189, 165 Cotter, Port Aransas.

Port Aransas Seafood Co. — (512) 749-5774, 2131 Park Rd., Port Aransas.

Port Aransas Historical Trail — Sponsored by local Boy Scout Troup 29. Those who complete it can earn a merit badge that depicts the historic lighthouse on the Lydia Ann Channel. Brochures detailing the trail can be found at the Chamber of Commerce. 14 points of interest are included with a brief description of each.

Horseback Riding — Mustang Riding Stable — (512) 749-5055 — Group Posses, hay rides, first timers, solo excursions. Located on Park Road 53 between Padre Island Drive and Port Aransas on Mustang Island.

Sightseeing — Scenic cruises are offered from Fisherman's Wharf aboard a catamaran with capacity for about 90 people. Trip is narrated and includes such points of interest as the lighthouse on the Lydia Ann Channel, the Brown and Root docks, the whooping cranes during their nesting season from November through March or April, and more. Call for times and fees. (512) 882-6161.

Surfing — Miles of the Gulf of Mexico await those who want to face the challenge of riding the surf. Surfboards and boogie boards are available for rent on the beach and at other locations in town.

Tennis — Many of the condominiums have tennis courts for their guests. Lighted public courts are open and free on the Port Aransas High School campus on Station Street just south of Beach Street.

Bingo — Three local organizations hold bingo for the public three nights a week. Tuesday, 7 P.M., at St. Joseph Catholic Church, 100 N. Station; Thursdays, 7 P.M., E.M.S. Ladies Auxiliary, Community Center on Alister Street; and Saturdays, 7 P.M., Ladies Fire Auxiliary, Community Center.

Annual Events: Outboard Fishing Tourney — July — (512) 749-5919.

Dean Hawn Fishing Tourney — July — (512) 749-5448.

Lighting of the Harbor — December — Santa Claus arrives by Coast Guard cutter in time for lighting of boats and businesses along waterfront; Christmas carol singalong, boat decoration contest, boat parade. In Texas, 1-800-242-3084 or U.S. 1-800-221-9198.

Black and Red Ball — February — (512) 749-5919.

Rotary Club Spaghetti Dinner — February — in Pollack Center. (512) 749-5919.

Port Aransas Wild Game and Seafood Dinner — March — Civic Center — "world famous dinner" hosted by Lion's Club, reservations recommended. 1-800-242-3084.

Spring Art Festival — Tarpon Inn Courtyard — April — (512) 749-5555.

A Taste of Port Aransas — May — Civic Center — finest in town's renowned restaurants offer tasty tidbits, soft drinks; Chinese auction in evening. Reservations recommended. (512) 749-5131.

Petticoat Fishing Tourney — June — for women only. (512) 749-5880.

National Championship of Port Aransas Bay Fishing Tourney — June — (512) 749-5252.

Gulf Coast Conservation Association Fishing Tourney —
June — (512) 749-5252.

Masters Fishing Tourney — (512) 749-5880.

Texas Championship Billfish Tourney — June. (512)
749-4100.

Island Moorings Billfish Tournament — July. (512) 749-
4100.

Powderpuff Fishing Tournament — July. (512) 749-5915.

Texas Women's Billfish Tourney — September. (512)
749-6998.

Port Aransas Day — September. (512) 749-5919.

Casino Night — October — at Civic Center. (512) 749-
4136.

Island Moorings Fall Fishing Tourney — October. (512)
749-4100.

Papa's Bay & Surf Fishing Tourney — October. (512)
749-5252.

EMS Chili Cookoff — October. (512) 749-5919.

MAKO Owners Fishing Tourney — August. (512) 749-
6624.

G.C.C.A Kingfish Tourney — August — Woody's. (512)
749-6624.

Deep Sea Roundup — July — One of Texas' largest, oldest fishing tournaments.

Sand Dune Regatta — (512) 884-5892.

Ladies Invitational Golf Tournament — August.

New Year's Eve Dance — 1-800-242-3084.

PORT LAVACA

Port Lavaca was once an old seaport, and today is a fisherman's resort. It began earlier as Linnville, which was
founded in 1831. The town was destroyed nine years later in a
Comanche raid that swept from the hills above Austin to the
coast. The following year Port Lavaca was built three miles
south of the original townsite. Lavaca means "cow" in Spanish, therefore, Port Lavaca means "port of the cow." Located

on the upper reaches of Matagorda Bay, deep sea fishing is quite good off-shore.

Points of Interest: Calhoun County Jail Museum — 301 S. Ann St. at Leona, two blocks south of Main. Free.

The original castle-like jail building is currently undergoing renovation. At the present time, the museum collection is located in Courthouse Annex at 201 W. Austin, right next door. Among the more interesting displays is a model of the townsite of Indianola as it looked in 1875 before a series of hurricanes permanently destroyed it. Open from 1:30 to 4:30 Tuesday through Friday. Once the jail building is reopened, hours will be 2–6 Tuesday through Thursday and 9–1 on Saturday.

Half Moon Reef Lighthouse — 2300 Texas 35, behind the Chamber of Commerce. The lighthouse was placed in operation in 1857. It once stood on Matagorda Bay and was moved near the causeway on Highway 35 next to the Port Lavaca Community Center. Until the Civil War, the lighthouse served as an aid to navigation for vessels coming in or out of the port towns of Lavaca and Indianola. In 1861, Confederates took control of the lighthouse and extinguished the light for the remainder of the Civil War. The light was relit on Feb. 20, 1868, and was active until repairs were made in 1885. Not open for a tour.

Port Lavaca — Off for the day

Lavaca Bay Causeway Bridge — Crosses Lavaca Bay and the 36-ft. Matagorda Ship Channel.

Port Lavaca Fishing Pier and State Park — This lighted pier is one of the longest in Texas and makes for pleasant walks as well as fishing. Includes public boat ramp, camping, playground, covered picnic tables, fishing.

Ranger Cemetery — Harbor St. off Broadway. Oldest cemetery in Calhoun County. Don't give up until you find it. It's hiding behind a fish cannery on the north side of the street. The cemetery was named after the 1850 burial of Margaret Peyton Lytle, the wife of the "poet" of the Texas Rangers. Major James Watts rests in the oldest grave. He was a victim of the Comanche raid of Linnville in 1840. Major Watts and his bride fled from the Indians, but Mrs. Watts insisted on returning to their home for a gold watch left behind. The Comanches murdered Watts, and captured his wife. Eventually a posse rescued Mrs. Watts. In the pursuit an Indian shot an arrow at her. She was saved when the arrow was deflected by the steel stays in her corset.

Bayfront Park — Extension of Main St. east of Broadway. (512) 552-9798. Free.

The site of the Blessing of the Fleet Celebration includes a playground that resembles a fort and covered picnic tables. Upcoming attractions include a marina.

Nautical Landings Marina.

La Salle's Cross — Grace Episcopal Church houses this cross, carried by La Salle when he landed at Indianola in 1685.

Port Lavaca Cemetery — Historical marker for Jefferson Beaumont located here.

88

Magnolia Beach — Beach activities, sailboard rentals, picnic tables, fishing, boat ramp.

Green Lake — The largest natural fresh water lake in Texas.

Hatch Bend Country Club — Golf, swimming, tennis and club house.

Guadalupe River — boat ramp and river development.

Antiques: A Little Bit Country — Highway 35 South.

Annual Events: Annual Season Opener Golf Tournament — March.

The Spring Art Show — April — Pastels, oils, watercolors, acrylics and sculptures are displayed at this judged show of regional artists, sponsoring both adult and youth categories.

Cinco de Mayo — May — Part of a state-wide celebration of Mexican history. Cinco de Mayo is highlighted in Port Lavaca with live music and food.

The Annual Seafood Golf Tournament — May — The Hatch Bend Country Club hosts this exciting 36-hole tournament on its excellent golf course. Included is a delicious seafood dinner with other golf enthusiasts.

The Calhoun County Youth Rodeo — June — This rodeo pits local youth against each other in a contest of riding and roping skills.

Juneteenth — June — Celebrated state-wide, Juneteenth in Calhoun County includes a beauty queen contest, special breakfast with speaker, ice cream freeze-off, bean cook-off, and fun and games including baseball and sack races.

Blessing of the Fleet — July — Sponsored by the Calhoun County Chamber of Commerce, this celebration is held in Port Lavaca the weekend before shrimp season begins. Area boats are outfitted with colorful decorations and paraded before a priest and visitors as the blessing is given, wishing the shrimpers a safe and bountiful season. The blessing is followed by a gumbo cook-off, arts and crafts booths, sand castle building contests, kite flying contest, fun run, and other activities.

The Ladies' Invitational Golf Tournament — August — This is a ladies-only golf event held at the beautiful Hatch Bend Country Club golf course.

Annual Lavaca Jaycee Labor Day Fishing Tournament —September — This weekend event for sport fishermen could result in one lucky person "hooking" a $10,000 prize for landing the specially tagged fish. Daily and grand prizes for winners in 5 categories are presented at the end of the tournament.

The Mexican Heritage Fiesta — September — Coinciding with the same ancestral festival in Mexico, the country celebration revolves around events such as a beauty queen contest, ballet folklorico, mariachis, pinatas, Mexican food, Menudo cook-off, street dance and low rider cars on display. (512) 552-2959.

The Chamber of Commerce Annual Consignment Auction — September — This is an opportunity to see or participate in an old fashioned auction, on items from farm equipment to antiques. (512) 552-2959.

The Annual Couples Golf Tournament — October.

The Calhoun County Fair and Junior Livestock Show — October — The fair is kicked-off on the Saturday before with "Go Texan Days," with barbeque, bean and chili cook-offs, and a dance. Held at the fair grounds, the county fair features a beauty queen contest, livestock judging and auction, Lady's Day Luncheon and Fashion Show, a large carnival and a parade in downtown Port Lavaca. (512) 552-2959.

Blue-winged Teal

Ducks Unlimited Banquet — October — As part of the National Ducks Unlimited, the local chapter helps raise money to preserve and restore breeding grounds of waterfowl in Canada and the northern U.S. Included are a delicious dinner, door prizes, auction, raffle and sale of Ducks Unlimited apparel.

The Lavaca Bay Arts and Crafts Festival — November — A Port Lavaca shopping mall provides the perfect showplace for the annual Art Guild arts and crafts show and sale, one of the finest in the area.

Taste of Heritage — July — Ethnic food and entertainment.

Texan Days — Barbecue, bean and chili cook-offs, and a dance. Held at the fair grounds, the county fair features a beauty queen contest, livestock judging and auction, Lady's Day Luncheon and Fashion Show, a variety of exhibits, a large carnival and a parade in downtown Port Lavaca. (512) 552-2959.

Texas Summerfest — June — 4-day event — dance, food booths, arts and crafts.

Festival of Lights — December — City-wide holiday celebration with events for all ages. Lighting of community tree and night parade. Victorian-style charity ball and dinner. Hospital auxiliary Christmas dance. Historical homes tour and "Masquerade on Main" Gala at the Station. (512) 552-4083.

The Chamber of Commerce Christmas Parade — December — This is the largest parade of the year and comes complete with beautifully decorated, colorful floats, horses and riders, the Shriners and marching bands.

Charter Boat Services: Bay Area Charter Service — 416 E. Railroad — (512) 552-3282.

Deep Blue Charters — P.O. Box 1181 — (512) 983-4232.

Doc's Dock — Kalie Charter — On the Intercoastal Canal — (512) 983-2621.

J & L Charter Service — P.O. Box 397 — (512) 983-2621.

Art Galleries: Art Crafts — 237 E. Main.

Live oak

Fresh Seafood Markets: Clark's Fish Market — 7th at Intercoastal Canal.

Evelyn's Fish Market — 732 Broadway.
Priddy's Oyster House — 614 Broadway.

PORT O'CONNOR

This jaunty little resort with a fresh quality has risen from several storms. Hurricane Carla almost totally destroyed it in 1961. Many years ago a wealthy man named Decros resided in a mansion on Decros Point across from Matagorda Island. He was determined to ride out a fierce hurricane and strapped his gold to his body. After the storm was over neither he nor his gold were ever seen again.

Port O'Connor originally began as a small settlement called Alligator Head. It was later renamed Port O'Connor in honor of Thomas O'Connor on whose original land grant it was located. A Confederate stronghold was once there named Fort Esperanza (Hope) and bluffed Federal warships off the pass with timber imitating big guns. The fort was abandoned and burned in 1863.

Points of Interest: Matagorda Lighthouse — The 1852 lighthouse is visible from the seaward tip of Port O'Connor.

Old Coast Guard Station — The ruins of a station that was supposedly hurricane proof.

Annual Events: Port O'Connor Memorial Day Fishing Tournament — May — Trophies and prizes and street dance highlight this Memorial weekend happening.

The Annual Port O'Connor Fourth of July Festival — July — This festival begins with a Texas-style barbeque and arts and crafts fair, and ends with a spectacular fireworks display set on the beach and reflected in the dark mirror of the water.

Port O'Connor — sails in the sunset
— Photo by Richard Siemens

Port O'Connor — shell hunters

Outdoor Writer's Tournament — June. Matagorda Island Adventure — April — Archaeology, beach ecology, birding, history, and nature hikes. Takes place in Matagorda Island State Park and Wildlife Management Area. Departure is Saturday A.M. A La Salle Feast is offered Saturday night featuring roast turkey and a rabbit-vegetable soup prepared in buffalo stock, corn on the cob, salad greens, and "Spoonbill Sorbet." After the feast, everyone is invited to gather around the campfire for visits by "Ghosts from Matagorda Island's Past," an outdoor drama. History tours will be offered to the Matagorda Island Lighthouse built in 1852 and to trenches dug by Confederate forces in 1862 in an effort to protect Pass Cavallo and the port of

94

Indianola from Union attack. Exhibits and lectures at the Visitor's Center on Saturday will describe the island's history, archaeology, and vulnerability to development. Birding, beach ecology and nature hikes led by naturalists will depart from the Visitor's Center at regular inter-

vals. Conditions on the island are for those more interested in adventure than in comfort.

Port O'Connor Used Boat Show — April — (512) 983-2898 — Arts and crafts, marine service, fishing, information, rod makers, fish fry.

The Poco Bueno Invitational Offshore Fishing Tournament — July — Held each year in Port O'Connor, this is the richest fishing tournament on the coast.

Crowds gather to the magnificent boats and excitement builds as the contestants come in to weigh their marlin or sailfish.

Deep Blue Charters — Offshore fishing and diving, bay fishing and island shuttles — (512)983-4232. Fish for seasonal king, ling, dolphin, barracuda, amberjack, tuna, shark, and red snapper (caught year-round).

Snapper Snatcher — Bay and gulf charters, island shuttle, duck and goose hunts — (512) 983-4447.

Seafood Markets: Raby's Seafood — famous stuffed crabs.

PORTLAND

Residents of Portland, Texas, share a mutual blessing. While all other cities in the world experience only four seasons, this community shares a fifth. Winter, spring, summer, fall, and FOOTBALL season occur here. Just as surely as winter brings icicles, spring brings flowers, summer brings surfboards, and fall brings hurricanes, out of FOOTBALL

Portland — Northshore Country Club

Portland — Northshore Country Club Golf Course

season emerges countless shaven heads, ace bandages, and a tidal wave of bright red and blue wardrobes, cars, banners, uniforms, and emotions. What a spectacle!!!

Sitting on a 39-foot bluff over-looking beautiful Corpus Christi and Nueces Bays, Portland was carved from a wilderness of thick brush and snake-infested plain. The original townsite covered  two square miles on land originally given by the Republic of Texas to veterans of the War for Independence from Mexico. Early investors were stockholders of land companies in Portland, Maine, and named the town in honor of their home-town. Professor T. M. Clark moved his family to Portland by train in 1894. He founded Bay View College, which was lo-cated on the east side of Portland. The hurricanes of 1916 and 1919 destroyed much of the town's businesses. Before the causeway to Corpus Christi was built, wagons forded across the Nueces Bay on an oyster reef.

 For years Gum Hollow was a favor-ite waterfowl haven for hunters the coun-try over. Gum Hollow was formed by an earthen dam that held water for stock. It was located at the dip in the West Port-land Road, Farm Road 893, about three miles west of town. The Coleman Fulton Pasture Company had built the dam. Every year, hundreds of ducks and geese swarmed to this place for the winter. At times, private railroad cars brought well-known hunters to "Gum Holler." E. H. R. Green (son of famous Hettie Green), Mark Twain, William Jennings Bryan and William Howard Taft all hunted there. Storms and rains finally washed the dam away. It is now nothing more than a slight arroyo still called "Gum Holler" by the old-timers.*

---

* *Portland: Pioneers to Present,* compiled by Portland Library Board, 1972.

Points of Interest: Birdwatching Pier — Located just north of Indian Point Pier. Nesting of many varieties of birds visible from this point. Playground, picnic area.

Dinah Bowman Studio and Gallery — 312 5th Avenue — (512) 643-4922. Established in 1979 in one of the oldest buildings in Portland. Dinah's studio is housed in a wooden frame building on a shellcrete foundation. Features watercolors, scratchboard, fish rubbings (gyotaku), and other media concentrating on many forms of marine life as well as birds and seashells. Drop by!!

Indian Point Pier — Ideal fishing off the north end of the causeway between Portland and Corpus Christi. Concession stand, admission.

Northshore Golf Course — One of the nation's largest and most beautiful golf courses sitting pretty on Corpus Christi Bay. Hosts several tournaments a year in both golf and tennis.

Annual Events: Christmas Tour of Homes — Sponsored by St. Christopher's by the Sea Episcopal Church. Several local homes are festively decorated in various motifs.

Windfest — April — (512) 643-2475 — Parade, golf tournament, arts & crafts, carnival, tennis tournament, 10-K run, style show, street dance, white elephant auction, sailboard race, cloggers, live bands, food booths.

Taste of Portland — February — (512) 643-2475.

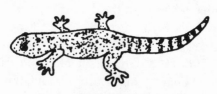

REFUGIO

Refugio, Anglos say (Re-fur-ee-o) *Tejanos* say (Re-fu-hi-o). In 1795 the Spanish built their last mission in Texas here in an attempt to Christianize the Karankawa. The Karankawa were a feared Indian tribe believed to be cannibalistic. The mission was called "La Mision de Nuestra Senora de Refugio" (The Mission of Our Lady of Refuge). It became a half-Irish, half-Mexican town in 1834 in the Power-Hewitson colony. Mexican General José Urrea and his forces captured the town during the Texas Revolution. Defenders were sent to join the prisoners  at Goliad and were later executed with them. The town has a lovely selection of old and historic buildings. Many date from the 1860s to the turn of the century, and range in style from primitive Greek Revival to large elaborate Victorians. Occasionally some of these buildings are open to the public for tours.

Points of Interest: City Park — Always open, free. Focal point is an eight-sided memorial rising 30 feet above a star-shaped floral garden, dedicated to heroes of the Texas Revolution.

Good Ship Lollipop Factory — Visiting Betty Norman's lollipop factory is a treat for anyone who stops. The lollipops are made from her original recipe daily. She insists on making small batches at a time. Keeping the batches small is one secret to these delicious, less than 200 calorie, lollipops. Tours through the kitchen are given where one can watch the process of pouring into molds, inserting sticks, cooling, chipping, cleaning, wrapping, and labelling. Lollipop trees are sold as well.

King's Park — Located in the town's original town square. The park is a memorial to King and his men, who lost their lives fighting for their independence from Mexico. There is a library and gazebo on the grounds. Other parks in Refugio are Lions' Shelly Park on the Mission River and Heritage Park, which has a ballpark complex and a public pool.

Refugio Soaring Circle — One of the oldest and largest glider clubs in the United States. Headquarters at the Refugio County Airport just south of Refugio off U.S. Highway 77. Provides early morning thermals that have lifted gliders toward several record breaking flights, including one from Refugio to Liberal, Kansas.

Refugio County Museum — 102 W. West. (512) 526-5555. Local artists give lessons periodically. Displays of interest, some permanent and some of special interest for timely events are shown.

Art Galleries: Geo-Gina's Art Gallery — 612 S. Alamo — (512) 526-4343 — Traditional and western art.

Vagabond Gallery of Art — 102 Purisima — (512) 526-2424 — Wide variety.

Annual Events: Refugio County Fair and Rodeo — March. Fairgrounds, Texas Highway 202 near U.S. Highway 183. (512) 526-2835. Free. An all-around rodeo with barrel racing and calf roping.

PRCA Refugio Pro Rodeo — March — County Fair Grounds — world-class pro cowboys competing for prize money in bull-riding, calf roping, steer wrestling, barrel racing.

Cutting Horse Competition — March, May–Oct. — Gulf Coast Cutting Horse Assoc. — O'Brien Rodeo Arena, Ref. Co. Fairgrounds.

Polo Exhibition & Casino Night — April — County Fairgrounds.

Annual Bobcat Relays — April.

Our Lady of Refuge Annual Easter Egg & Bake Sale, Sunrise Service — April.

Refugio County Texas Youth Rodeo — May — County Fairgrounds.

Annual Refugio County Crops Tour — June.

Annual Benefit Golf Tournament — Refugio Chamber of Commerce — August — Refugio Country Club.

Pachanga — Annual Arts & Crafts Festival — Sept. — music, jugglers, ballet folklorico, dance — King's Park.

Annual Bizarre Bazaar — Oct. — trade fair for unusual birds & animals — Refugio County Community Center.

Annual Food & Fashion Show — Refugio Co. Chamber of Commerce.

"Home for Christmas" festival — Dec. — nine days of activities and entertainment.

Blackland Emporium — 231 Green Ave. (512) 528-2136.

RIVIERA

Riviera (Ri-ver-a) is a village near the head of Baffin Bay. In 1568 three English sailors, survivors of Sir John Hawkins' raiders trapped in Vera Cruz, supposedly walked northward to ultimate rescue aboard an English ship in Canadian waters. Their disputed report noted vegetation at the Rio Grande, as well as this indented coastline. It is near this area that an Indian burial ground of the Karankawa Indians has been found. The Indians nursed and enslaved Spanish explorer Cabeza de Vaca after his shipwreck in 1528. In 1927 archaeologists excavated over 20 skeletons, burned human bones (suggesting ritual cannibalism), potsherds, arrowpoints, flint tools, fire implements, and shells. The Karankawa Indians were unusually tall and muscular. They tattooed their bodies and smeared themselves with alligator grease to keep off insects.

Points of Interest: Kaufer-Hubert Memorial Park — Located at the end of FM Rd. 628 — campgrounds, fishing, picnic shelters, lakes, restrooms, observation tower, lighted pier, boat ramp, sandy beach with shower, birding overlook, jogging trail, playgrounds, horseshoe pits, soccer/softball fields.

Sea Wind Resort — Located beside the Kaufer-Hubert Memorial Park — offers RV sites, restroom/showers, recreation room, planned activities.

Brush Country Inn — World famous for its Chicken Fried Steak. Located on Highway 77.

The Barn Door Restaurant and Gift Shop — Hwy. 77. Good food as well as antique displays that are for sale.

Sarita Safaris, Inc. — Located south of Riviera — offers day lease hunting services. Includes bird hunts, deer and exotics. (512) 294-5291.

King's Inn Restaurant — Noted for its family style serving of fresh, fried seafood. Not uncommon for folks to drive a hundred miles to eat at this well-loved restaurant.

ROBSTOWN

This city is a great jumping off place to just about any sport you might enjoy. Freshwater fishing at nearby Lake Corpus Christi and saltwater fishing in the Gulf are readily

Robstown — Art Festival

available. For the hunter, ducks are plentiful and local folks helpful about where to find them. Easy access to malls at the south end of Corpus Christi makes shopping a pleasure. Don't miss Cotten's Bar-B-Que, if you can help it.

About 1905, Bob Driscoll succeeded in obtaining a permit for the Texas-Mexican Railroad from Laredo to Corpus Christi. Soon afterwards the Missouri-Pacific tracks were laid from St. Louis to Brownsville, crossing the Texas-Mexican track. Since all the land in the area was owned by the Driscoll family, Robert Driscoll started a store at the intersection, which was called Rob's Town, later Robstown. Cotton is a major cash crop.

ROCKPORT

When you head toward the Rockport-Fulton area you've taken the first step towards the discovery of a truly unique Texas coastal retreat.

The Spanish first explored the area in 1519. The French tried to settle here in the 1720s with overwhelming resistance from the Karankawa Indians. The notorious pirate Jean LaFitte built a fort nearby in the early 1800s. General Zachary Taylor's army camped here in 1845 during the Mexican War.

In more recent times, visitors to this area have discovered an environment they never knew existed in Texas: windswept oak trees, the charm of a New England fishing village, quaint shops  and fabulous restaurants that serve fresh seafood from the bay. Rockport is also one of the homes of the nearly extinct Whooping Crane.

Rockport — Art Center

Rockport Harbor by Night
— Photo by Richard Siemens

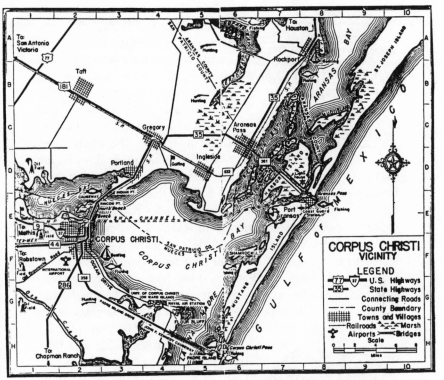

Points of Interest: Aransas National Wildlife Refuge — The Refuge is about 38 miles north of Rockport and known world-wide as the winter home of the endangered Whooping Cranes. Visitors can see the birds from an observation tower in the park or by boat that leaves from the Rockport-Fulton area October to April. Park opens daily 8 to

5. Museum, picnic sites, trails. Rookery tours April to July. Admission $2/car.

The Big Tree — On the Texas Gulf Coast, protected from man but not from the elements of nature. It is the largest live

oak in Texas. It is located about 10 miles north of Rockport, in the Goose Island State Park. Signs inside the park direct visitors to the tree. The mammoth live oak is sometimes referred to as the "Bishop's Tree," because a Catholic Bishop's home or chapel stood nearby in the abandoned townsite of Lamar. The name "Lamar Oak" was probably obtained from this town, which flourished in the 1830s. Legend has it that the Goose Island Oak was once a place where cannibalistic Karankawas held councils and pagan ceremonies in which they devoured their enemies and even members of their own tribe. It is also referred to as a hanging tree and as a rendezvous of the fierce Comanche Indians. In 1966 this state champion live oak measured 431$\frac{1}{4}$ inches at its circumference, was 44 feet high, and it had a crown spread of 89 feet. Its age has never been accurately determined but it is believed to be at least 2,000 years old.

Earlier visitors to this area may have included the Spanish explorer Cabeza de Vaca in 1528, Sieur de La Salle in 1684, and Governor Alonso de Leon, who came in 1689 to find La Salle but found instead the ruins of St. Louis and rescued the only three survivors of La Salle's colony from the Karankawas.

Swiss Chocolate Villa — Hwy. 35 between Rockport and Fulton — This establishment is Swiss-owned. It features handmade chocolate and diabetic candies in every shape, form, or fashion imaginable.

Fulton Mansion State Historic Structure — Located off State Highway 35, three miles north of Rockport, at the corner of Henderson Street and Fulton Beach Road. The Fulton Mansion overlooks Aransas Bay in the resort towns of Rockport-Fulton, 30 miles north of Corpus Christi, Texas. Built in the mid-1870s, this French Second Empire mansion with its mansard roof must have appeared other-worldly, rising from the flat terrain of sparsely populated Live Oak Peninsula. With its unusual architecture and stylish interiors, the mansion displays the exceptional talents and tastes of its builder, George Ware Fulton. The Fulton Mansion is open for guided tours Wednesday  through Sunday, 9:00 A.M. to noon and 1:00 P.M. to 4:00 P.M. — last tour in the morning, 11:30, last tour in the afternoon, 3:30; closed Christmas Day. Admission is $2 for adults and $1 for children ages 6 to 12, under 6 free. Groups of 10 or more are requested to make reservations at least one month in advance of their visit. Visitors are requested to wear flat, soft-soled shoes to prevent damage to carpets and floors. The first floor and basement are accessible to the handicapped. The Fulton Mansion is operated by the Texas Parks and Wildlife Department with assistance from the Fulton Mansion Docent organization, a dedicated group of volunteers.

Goose Island State Park — Contains picnic sites, shelters, camping and R.V. sites, trails, boat launch, fishing pier, group pavilion and playground. State Park user fees.

Historic Homes — Although the homes listed here are not open to the public, their varied and interesting architecture make this an interesting driving tour.

1. 617 South Water — Built in 1868 by John W. Baylor, a wealthy cattleman. This home, built of cedar construction, has withstood over a century of hurricane pounding. Some imperfect glass in the doors and windows is original. All of the flooring, the doorknobs, walls, and most of the outside shutters are original.

2. The Mathis Home — 621 South Church. The Mathis home was built in 1869–70 by T. H. Mathis, cattle baron. The cypress from which the house was built was imported. The foundation is 7-foot brick arches. Much of the fence still has original cypress balusters. The home is now owned by a descendant of the builder. There are many family heirlooms

throughout the home, including one of the original cattle brands from the Coleman, Mathis, and Fulton Pasture Company, once one of the leading industries of the area.

3. South on Church Street are several homes dating from the 1880s and 1890s. The tiny tin-roofed building at 702 S. Church was once the Methodist Parsonage. The gray home at 712 S. Church was built in the early 1890s, abandoned  about 50 years and recently restored. Across the street at 717 S. Church, the blue home was built late in 1880 by Charles Bailey. He was the owner of the first newspaper in the county and also owned an over-the-water pavilion. The home stayed in the family until the mid-1970s. The two-story gray home at 801 S. Church was built originally on Austin Street in 1874 by Judge Hynes. It was moved to this location in 1906 and the second story was added. Cypress and Louisiana pine were used in its construction. The home has been restored after damage by 1970 storms. One block west of the Bailey home is a city park where General Zachary Taylor's army camped on the way to Mexico in 1845.

4. Central Area Historic Home — At 509 S. Live Oak is a home recently rebuilt. It was originally built in 1880 in "Oklahoma" — a community 2 miles south of this location. When Oklahoma failed, the home was moved by barge to its present site. The home was the home of the first child born in Aransas County, David Rock Scrivener, born 1868, who with his wife lived here for many years. The R. H. Wood home at 203 N. Magnolia was built in the winter of 1867–68. His son, William W. Wood, was born here in 1871. Col. John H. Wood, father of R. H., was one of the founders of Rockport and a leader in industry. The L. M. Bracht home at 902 Cornwall was built in Oklahoma in 1881 by F. C. Finney, the developer. The Brachts moved the home here in 1889. The R. M. Bracht home at Magnolia and Concho was built in 1885. It was re-

modeled after the 1970 storm and again after a 1985 fire. One of the homes that A. L. Bruhl, a prominent druggist, owned is now located at 910 Concho after being moved from the corner of Allen and Nopal.

5. The Cape Cod Style Home across from the Chamber of Commerce was built in 1868 by Judge Williamson Moses. It was bought in 1872 by James C. Fulton, son of George W. Fulton. The home is still owned by a descendant of the family. The home is of cypress and Florida pine.

Fulton Beach — Harbor, public pier and swimming beach as well as site of the "Paws & Taws" building, home of the Rockport/Fulton Tourist Association. The local AARP Chapter meets here.

Lamar Historical Cemetery — The Lamar Cemetery originally served pioneer settlers of the Lamar community founded by James W. Byrne, a native of Ireland and a veteran of the Texas Revolution. It was named for his friend Mirabeau B. Lamar, former President of the Republic of Texas. The earliest grave is that of Patrick O'Connor, a direct descendant of Roderick O'Connor, the last King of Ireland.

Lyndon Baines Johnson Causeway Fishing Piers — Divides Copano Bay from Aransas Bay. The ends of the old causeway are now two of the longest lighted piers for fishing in the world. Operated by the Texas Parks and Wildlife Dept., there is a small fee to fish. Free boat launch.

Marion Packing Co. — Across Fulton Beach Road at the intersection of Chaparral are the ruins of the Marion Packing Company. About twenty packing companies once existed in the general area during the 1860s to 1880s.

Rockport Art Center — Home of Rockport Art Association, Inc. It is the blue building by the Rockport Harbor. This was a home originally built in 1890 by Bruhl O'Connor and located at 901 Broadway. It has been redesigned to house three studio classrooms and four gallery display areas. The

Rockport — Roseate Spoonbill
— Photo by David Blankinship

home was donated to the Art Association by Tom O'Connor in 1982. It is open Tuesday thru Saturday 10 to 5 and Sundays 2 to 5 for art exhibit viewing. The purpose of the Center is to provide youth and adult art education, to promote and stimulate local and South Texas art, and provide public display of quality artwork.

Sisters of Schoenstatt Convent — A haven for religious renewal and spiritual formation. The retreat center includes the Schoenstatt Shrine and Convent. It is located at Goose Island, 10 miles outside Rockport. The Sisters minister in parochial positions and serve as teachers, family counselors, social workers or work in health care settings. The main task of the Sisters is their work at the Schoenstatt Movement.

Rockport Beach Park — This beach is a one and one-quarter mile sandy beach projecting from the Rockport Harbor. The beach is ideal for shallow swimming with two lifeguarded swimming areas, one being a salt water pool. One end of the beach is reserved for waterskiing and boating. There is a 360-foot shoreline pier next to a four-lane boat ramp designated for powerboats and a separate launch for small sailboats. Water sport rentals, including paddleboats and jet skis, are also available in this area. On the beach is an 800-foot fishing pier, two park pavilions with restroom facilities and a store for added convenience. Not only does the beach provide swimming, waterskiing and boating, but also excellent bird watching on the coast. An elevated observation platform has been built to accommodate birdwatchers. Beachgoers do not have to worry about parking since plenty of space is available.

Texas Maritime Museum — In the fall of 1988 the state's first official maritime museum broke ground to begin its structure at Rockport/Fulton on the Texas Gulf Coast. The Texas Maritime Museum is now open. (512) 729-1271.

Veteran's Memorial — Located at the corner of Austin and S. Navigation Circle. Dedicated Nov. 11, 1984, it honors Aransas County's war dead from WWII through Viet Nam.

Zachary Taylor Oak — Located at the southeast corner of South Pearl Street and Bay Street. A bronze and concrete marker was placed near the base of the tree to commemorate the place where Brigadier General Zachary Taylor, Commander of the U.S. Army, camped until returning to St. Joseph Island.

Annual Events: Fulton Oysterfest — First weekend in March — P.O. Box 501, Fulton, 78378, (512) 729-7529. Features food booths, oyster eating and shucking contests, and arts and crafts.

Rockport Art Festival — Fourth of July weekend, P.O. Box 987, Rockport, 78382, (512) 729-5519. Auction, foods, live entertainment. This festival is of special interest to many visitors. It showcases the talents of hundreds of artists from Texas and outside state lines.

Rockport Seafair — Weekend preceding Columbus Day

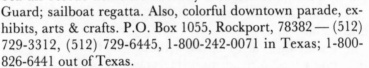

— Two full days of fun, feast and frolic. Fresh-from-the-bay seafood served continuously all weekend; shrimp, oysters, crab and fish with plenty of country-style hushpuppies and corn on the cob. Featured event is World Championship Gumbo Cookoff where anxious cooks try their hands at concocting winning recipes of seafood, spices and sauces. Boat parade with every type of vessel, including world and pleasure boats, barges, dinghies and yachts. Sea-air rescue demonstration by U.S. Coast Guard; sailboat regatta. Also, colorful downtown parade, exhibits, arts & crafts. P.O. Box 1055, Rockport, 78382 — (512) 729-3312, (512) 729-6445, 1-800-242-0071 in Texas; 1-800-826-6441 out of Texas.

Recreation: Golf — Many visitors belonging to the USGA-affiliated golf clubs enjoy reciprocal privileges at Rockport Country Club and Live Oak Country Club.

Ornithology Anyone? — The stately whooping crane, a seriously endangered species, is making a welcome comeback. Local residents are rightfully proud that the cranes spend their winter months at nearby Aransas Wildlife Ref-

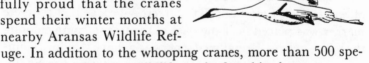

uge. In addition to the whooping cranes, more than 500 species of birds and other wildlife can be found in the area.

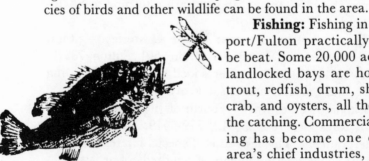

Fishing: Fishing in Rockport/Fulton practically can't be beat. Some 20,000 acres of landlocked bays are home to trout, redfish, drum, shrimp, crab, and oysters, all there for the catching. Commercial fishing has become one of the area's chief industries, bringing in millions of pounds of shrimp and fish each year, much of which is processed and shipped to other parts of the nation.

Water Sports: Take your pick: swimming, boating, waterskiing, jet skiing, sailing, windsurfing.

RUNGE

Established around 1850 as a trading post.
Runge Fun-fest — April.

SAN PATRICIO

San Patricio, settled by Irish colonists in the 1920s, today is constructing replicas of some of the oldest buildings in the area. Included in this reconstruction is the old county courthouse. The oldest cemetery in South Texas is here. (See Cemeteries)

Points of Interest: Dougherty House — Built in 1876 by Robert Dougherty, it once housed an academy for boys. At that time the two-story house afforded a classroom on the second floor with bedrooms to accommodate the boarding students who came from Mexico to attend the school. After Mr. Dougherty's health failed in 1881, his daughter, Kate Bluntzer, continued the school as a public school for several years. It is located at Round Lake, some $2^1/_2$ miles northwest of San Patricio. The home was designed in the manner of a house in Ireland, much admired by Mr. Dougherty. Porticos are on two sides of the house, one facing the lake. Stickwork has been added through the years to trim the porticos and the large gallery at the rear. It bears the official Texas Historical Commission's marker and is maintained by the Dougherty Historical Foundation. Tours are available on special occasions.

McGloin House — This lovely structure is the only remaining Empresario's home in Texas. James McGloin built it

113

San Patricio — Feeding cattle

in 1855. The exterior is white with green shutters, trim and lattice work. The story-and-a-half house with two dormer windows overlooks Round Lake. Anaqua and mulberry trees, planted by the couple along the lane, still stand today. Mr. McGloin and his second wife Mary Murphy lived in the house one year until his death. He was buried from the house, and an Irish wake was held in the front room. His nephew Patrick McGloin's family and descendants lived there for many years. Several folk tales and ghost stories are centered around the area. In 1853 James McGloin saw the bloodied ghost of his father-in-law and partner John McMullen. After seeing the apparition, McGloin saddled his horse and rode to San Antonio where McMullen lived. Upon arriving, he learned McMullen had been stabbed to death as he slept. His nephew's wife, Mary Ann McGloin, viewed the "Lady in Green" skimming across the surface of Round Lake in 1874. The apparition, wearing a green dress, is thought to be the girl he left behind in Ireland. The McGloin Homestead and grounds are available to groups for meetings, field trips, and picnics. (512) 992-6003.

Rattlesnake Races — March.
St. Patrick's Day — March.

SEADRIFT

This colorful city derives its name from all the driftwood that washes ashore there, coming down from the Guadalupe River into San Antonio Bay. Long ago, residents with wood burning stoves got their wood there. Seadrift enjoys lovely sunsets in an area rich with mesquite, lantana, and oleander trees. The Yucca plant (Spanish Dagger) and Century Plant is found locally and blossoms beautifully in spring.

Bayfront Park — covered picnic tables, tour of refuge, observation tower, indoor educational animal display.

Festivals: The Annual Seadrift Oyster Shucking Contest — April — This is a fast-paced contest be-

Range — Horned Lizard

115

tween professional shuckers to see who can open the most oysters in the least time. Other activities include a fried oyster dinner, oyster on the half shell, an oyster eating contest, oyster races, races, recipe contest, and information about oysters and the industry.

The Texas Water Safari Race — June — This historic canoe race is the world's toughest boat race. It begins in San Marcos and ends in Seadrift. It is a non-stop 260 miles by muscle-powered boats and is a grueling test of skill and stamina.

Shrimpfest — July — (512) 785-2309. Fourth of July weekend festival which celebrates the shrimp season with a candlelight blessing of the fleet, queen contest, arts & crafts fair, boiled shrimp dinner, fun run, fiddler contest, street dance, 16-mile canoe race, sailboat races and other exciting activities.

SCHROEDER

This town was named Germantown until WWI. The local people objected to the name of the town and decided to rename it after the first person who had been killed in World War I from that town. His name was Schroeder.

Trail ride — First Saturday in February to the San Antonio Live Stock Show.

Schroeder — cactus bloom

— Photo by Richard Siemens

Sinton — County Courthouse

117

SINTON

Sinton was named for David Sinton of Cincinnati, Ohio, who bought 51% of Coleman-Fulton Pasture Co. His ranch headquarters on Chiltipin Creek became the townsite. It is a windy little city of many parks and is the county seat of San Patricio.

Points of Interest: Country Cornerstone — 102 E. Sinton — (512) 364-5756 — Co-op featuring local handmade items.

Welder Park — public park with golf course, picnic facilities and pavilions. Located off Hwy. 181. Large oak trees.

Rob and Bessie Welder Wildlife Foundation — (512) 364-2307 — A nonprofit institution to wildlife research and education. It was founded through a bequest in the will of the late Rob H. Welder. Admission by reservation. Restrooms and water fountains available. Entrance is on the east side of the Missouri-Pacific Railroad tracks, along U.S. Hwy. 77, approximately 7.4 miles northest of  Sinton, or 11 miles southwest of Woodsboro. Tour groups are admitted each Thursday afternoon, except for holidays, between 2:55 and 3:00 o'clock. Gates are locked at all other times. Tours require up to 2½ hours, depending on weather conditions and other factors. Schedule normally includes inspection of the Foundation Museum and other facilities, a discussion and slide program of the Foundation's objectives and research, and a tour of a portion of the refuge area. Visitors provide their own transportation on tours, which normally cover a total of eight to ten miles. Because of locked gates, visitors should plan to remain for the complete tour. Earlier departures can be arranged in case of emergency.

Annual Events: Old Fiddler's Festival — October — Held the last weekend in October each year, this is one festival you should catch. There is a little bit of everything, including fiddler's contest, costume contest, organ grinder, U.S. static display of military weapons, chili cookoff, South Texas Country Cloggers, hula dancers, square dancers, bands, gospel

Sinton — Veteran's Memorial

Sinton — Rob and Bessie Welder Park

119

music, volleyball tournament, cabrito cookoff, brisket cookoff, arts and crafts, and fancy shooting display. Parking $2 per vehicle. (512) 364-0327.

San Pat County A&H Youth Fund Dinner and Dance — November.

Santa Claus Comes to Sinton — December — Jackson Square, hot chocolate, pictures with Santa and carollers from the local church are usually on hand.

San Patricio County A&H Show Auction — January.

Chamber of Commerce Auction — Usually in the spring.

TYRA Youth Rodeo — June — (512) 364-3641.

SKIDMORE

Named for cattleman Frank O. Skidmore.

Skidmore

Skidmore — Museum

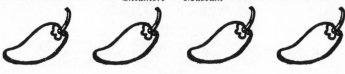

TAFT

Taft lays claim to being the "friendliest cotton-pickin' town in Texas." Trails coast-weathered homes and business houses along a highway lined by wind-whipped palms. Taft was once the center of the million-acre Taft Ranch, owned by the half-brother of President William Howard Taft. Taft boasts some of Texas' richest land. Cotton, oil and gas are the mainstay of the community.

Collector's Museum & Market — 113 Green Ave. (512) 528-3353.

Blackland Museum — Thursday, 10–12, and 1–4, and Sundays 2–5. Will open by special appointment for groups.

Blackland Emporium — 231 Green Ave. (512) 528-2136.

Taft Public Library — Houses some interesting paintings of the old Taft Ranch.

Taft — Welcome Sign

THREE RIVERS

Originally named Hamiltonberg, the U.S. Post Office renamed it Three Rivers because of its close proximity to the fork of the Nueces, Atascosa and Frio Rivers. Three Rivers' most outstanding feature is Choke Canyon Dam. A wide variety of wildlife inhabit the area, including the American Alligator, Rio Grande turkey, whitetail deer, javelina, coyote, opossum, fox, squirrel, raccoon, and various skunks. Fish found in the reservoir are largemouth bass, white bass, striped bass, crappie, bluegill, longear sunfish, green sunfish, flathead, channel and blue catfish, carp, freshwater drum and gar.

"Captain Crappiethoner"

Three Rivers — Prickly Pear Cactus
— Photo by Richard Siemens

Choke Canyon Reservoir — Provides camp sites, screened shelters, picnic areas, tennis and basketball courts, gymnasium, and dining hall, at the Calliham Unit. The south Shore Unit provides campsites, boat launches and picnic facilities. All areas offer excellent fishing and water skiing. It is located approximately 3.5 miles west of Three Rivers, along Texas Highway 72 to Tilden. The canyon was named for the steep banks of resistant rocks near the dam site which "choked" the Frio River during floods. Numerous archaeological sites in this area have been recorded. The Coahuiltecan Indians lived in the area. They were hardy, adaptable people and were recruited by Franciscan missionaries to work as agricultural laborers on mission farms. The promise of protection from Apaches and steady food supply brought their devotion, particularly in the winter months. Unfortunately, the Coahuiltecans lacked immunity to common childhood diseases, such as measles or chicken pox. These European-introduced diseases greatly reduced their number.

Tips State Recreation Park — 31 acre park one mile west off Texas 72 on the Frio River. Camping, fishing, picnic area.

Annual Event: Crappiethon U.S.A. — February — April — Small Entry Fee — big, big stakes!! Prizes are many and varied. Prizes as large as $60,000 are given away yearly. Bait up and get serious, folks!

ᚢ H.C. ᚤ ᚳᚫ ᚴ

TILDEN

Small mesquite-shaded town. Settled in 1858 as Rio Frio. Later called "Dog Town" because ranchers used many dogs to round up cattle. In 1871 the town was laid out as Colfax. Later it was renamed for S. J. Tilden, who won popular vote for U.S. President, 1876. The settlement, attempted in the 1860s, was abandoned because of violent banditry throughout the brush country. Vigilantes finally cleared the area. An old smugglers' trail from Laredo to San Antonio passed through the area. The operations of the outlaws gave rise to many stories of buried treasure. J. Frank Dobie, a one-time resident of

Tilden — Ranunculus

124

Tilden and popular historian, made the brush country of the late 19th century well known through his numerous books.

Stringfield Massacre — Thomas W. Stringfield family was ambushed by Indians and bandits raiding from Mexico, on September 28, 1870. Overtaken in their horse-drawn wagon, the victims ran for a nearby house, but did not reach it. Thomas, wife Sarah, and their six-year-old son, Adolphus, were murdered. The fate of Thomas, 4 years, was never known. Eight-year-old Ida Alice, fought to avoid capture. She was then speared 7 times, trampled by the raiders' horses and left for dead. She survived, was later rescued, and lived until 1937.

TIVOLI

Tivoli was platted in 1907 by J. W. Ward. The Refugio Land and Irrigation Company provided the community with a church, school, store, hotel, and cotton gin and mill. North of Tivoli are extensive freshwater marshes of the Guadalupe River Delta.

Tivoli — Alligator Gar

VICTORIA

This charming city is a blend of the past, the present, and the future. The city's older sections are lined with proud old homes, some dating back to the pre-Civil War era. Throughout the city, stately examples of historic architecture contrast with modern shopping malls, medical facilities, and educational facilities of higher learning. Something is usually happening here, both outdoors and in. Victoria was established by Spaniard Don Martin de Leon in 1824. The town lies eighty-five miles north of Corpus Christi, situated on the Guadalupe River.

Points of Interest: Cultural Council of Victoria — City Hall, 105 E. Juan Linn, (512) 572-ARTS. Information pertaining to season performances, exhibits, and ticket information can be obtained for all cultural events, including Victoria Symphony Orchestra, Victoria Community Theatre, Victoria Civic Chorus, Victoria Bach Festival Association, Victoria Summer Repertory Theater.

DeLeon Plaza — Main and Forrest Streets, (512)572-2763. Features shade trees, benches, gazebo, Six Flags and historic memorials.

McNamara House — 502 N. Liberty, (512) 575-8227. Contains period rooms and local history exhibits with a back gallery featuring changing exhibitions of local arts and crafts.

Memorial Square — 400 E. Commercial St. Wheeler. This is the oldest cemetery in Victoria and contains graves of some of the pioneer families of the city. An old steam engine that once belonged

126

Victoria — Proctor Building, Downtown and Main

Victoria — St. Mary's Catholic Church

127

to the Southern Pacific Railroad is on display. The Old Dutch wind grist mill contains two grinding stones brought from Norway to Indianola and inland by ox-cart before 1860.

Nave Museum — 306 W. Commercial, (512) 575-8227. Presents changing fine arts exhibitions. Owns a permanent collection of paintings by Royston Nave in whose memory the museum was built.

Riverside Park — 562 acres of woodland, bordered by four and one-half miles of the Guadalupe River. Provides tables, barbecue pits, benches, playground equipment, boat ramp, rose garden, exercise trail, hiking areas, duck pond.

Saxet Lakes Park — 95-acre park, 2 miles south of city limits on Highway 59, on Timberline Drive at Fordyce and Fox Roads. Fishing, swimming, picnic tables, pits, boat ramp, restrooms. 6 to sunset daily.

The Texas Zoo — Nestled among the native pecan trees in Victoria's Riverside Park on Stanton Street, between Red River and Vine. Open daily 10–5 except Thanksgiving, Christmas, New Year's Day. This zoo is young, but growing. Consists exclusively of animals native to Texas, allowing the opportunity for people to observe native Texas wildlife at close range. Conducts special fundraising and promotional events including Zoofest, Running Wild for the Texas Zoo, Owl Prowl, and Sundays Zoopreme.

Victoria County Courthouse — Bridge at Constitution Streets — Built in 1892 in Romanesque architecture by James R. Gordan in the style of Henry Richardson. The structure is made of Texas granite and Indiana limestone. It served as the seat of the county government from January 1893 to May 1967. The second-floor district courtroom has been fully restored as a reminder of times past, when spectacular court cases focused attention in a fine old building. Group tours available.

Coleto Creek Reservoir and Regional Park — (512) 575-6366. 33 spaces, water, electricity, dump station, showers, restrooms, pavilion by reservation, picnic tables, BBQ pits.

Golf — Riverside Golf Course features beautiful trees bordering all fairways.

Recreational Vehicle Park — Near Highway 87 North at Red River and Vine Streets, the park works on the honor system at $6.00 per night. Each of the 18 sites offers full hookups: water, electricity and sewer.

Annual Events: PRCA Rodeo — June — Community Center — (512) 573-5141.

Jaycees Stock Show — March — Community Center — parade, stock show, carnival, stock auction — (512) 575-0633.

Women's Clubhouse Spring Bazaar — March — Women's Clubhouse — (512) 573-4441.

Wild West Revue Arts & Crafts Show — March — Victoria Mall — (512) 576-1291.

Victoria Games Party — March — Knights of Columbus Hall — (512) 575-8524.

Invitation to the Dance — March — City's symphony orchestra at Victoria College Auditorium — (512) 576-4500.

Arts & Crafts Show — March — Town Plaza Mall (512) 574-5378 or 572-4618.

Symphonic Showpieces — May — City's symphony orchestra at Victoria College Auditorium — (512) 576-4600.

Paperback Book Sale — May — Bronte Room at public library — benefit sponsored by Friends of the Library — (512) 578-5329.

Antique Car Show — June — Victoria Mall — (512) 576-1291.

Miller Blastoff Fireworks Show — July — (512) 573-2401.

Country Arts & Crafts Fair — Begins end of June and extends into May — Victoria Mall — (512) 576-1291.

Coin Show — May — At Holiday Inn — (512) 575-0259.

Arts & Crafts Show — May — at Town Plaza Mall — (512) 578-0508.

South Texas Farm & Ranch Show — May — at Community Center — (512) 575-4581.

Fine Arts Festival — April — Town Plaza Mall — (512) 578-6555.

Jazz it up Home & Energy Show — Victoria Mall — (512) 576-1291.

International Armadillo Confab and Exposition — July — Festival spoof at DeLeon Plaza. Games, foods, arts and crafts, continuous entertainment — (512) 573-5277.

Running Wild for the Texas Zoo — July — 5-K run at Riverside Park — (512) 573-7681.

American International Circus Performances — August — Victoria Mall — (512) 573-7681.

Zoofest — August — Festival with Czech theme at Riverside Park — (512) 573-7681.

National Frisbee Contest Championship — August — (512) 573-2401.

Home Products Show — August — At Community Center — (512) 578-7711.

Victoria Bach Festival — June — (512)578-1297. First United Methodist Church. Wed. and Thurs., at Victoria College Auditorium, Fri. and Sat.

Hello Follies — June — (512) 387-2308.

VASA-CASA Chili & Barbeque Cookoff — August — Riverside Park — (512) 573-7603.

Balloon Extravaganza — September — (512) 578-3623.

Super Bowl of Chili — September — Riverside Park — (512) 575-2282.

Craft & Collectible Show — September — Avon Collectors Club at Holiday Inn — (512) 576-2123.

Gem & Jewelry Show — September — Sponsored by Gem & Mineral Society at Community Center — (512) 575-1825 or 578-8900.

Autofest — October — Victoria Mall — (512) 576-1291.

Czech Heritage Festival — October — Bluebonnet Convention Center — (512) 575-4581.

Taste the Midcoast — October — Area restaurants show off house specialties and host a dance at the Community Center — (512) 574-0015.

Crossroads Gun & Knife Show — October — in Knights of Columbus Hall (512) 573-2744.

10-K Run — November — (512) 573-6321.

Christmas in November Arts & Crafts Show — Community Center — (512) 575-4656.

Victoria Fest — (512) 573-5277 — November.

Symphony Concert — (512) 572-4425.

Sneak Preview of Santa's Workshop — December — Arts & Crafts show at Town Plaza Mall — (512) 575-8826.

Traditions — A Christmas Homes Tour — December — Three of the city's loveliest homes filled with Christmas cheer and family traditions; lunch served at Plaza Club. Benefits hospice organizations — (512) 578-6828.

WEESATCHE

About 15 miles north of the city of Goliad, there is a small town known as Weesatche. It was established in the late 1840s. For a period of time it was known as Middletown, because it was halfway between Goliad and Clinton. It was named after a local tree, the huisache, which is very common in the area.

Annual Events: Annual Fourth of July Feast — began in 1953 to make money to purchase the town's first fire truck and was popular enough to keep the tradition going.

Weesatche Big Buck Contest — A "Supper" takes place at the beginning of the season and an Award Dinner about the

Weesatche — wildflowers

second week in January. Bucks must be killed in Goliad or surrounding counties. Prizes are given for the 3 best Bucks, Longest Spike, Freak Horns, and the Best in the Youth Class. Held at the Weesatche Community Center.

WOODSBORO

Settled in the early 1900s by Czechs. Rich in agriculture. Nearby Mission River provides a popular water skiing area, but watch out for alligators which are plentiful. Tradition insists that a treasure-laden pirate sloop was driven ashore by a storm, and its booty is still awaiting some ambitious digger.

YORKTOWN

Yorktown was founded in 1848 as a way station on Old Indianola Trail. Captain John York commanded a company of Rangers at the capture of San Antonio in 1835. Yorktown, named in his honor, was laid out in 1848 on his land. Captain York was killed by Indians that same year. The town prospered as a center of farming and ranching; later of oil and gas.

City Park — Golf (512) 564-9191, tennis (512) 564-2611.

Yorktown Historical Museum — W. Main and Eckhardt Sts. — Open Mar.–Nov., Sun.–Thurs. 3–5 P.M.; Dec.–Feb., Sun., Thurs. 2–5 P.M. (512) 564-2661.

Annual Events: Stock Show — Held the 3rd weekend in February.

Western Days — 3rd weekend in October every fall. Street dance, arts & crafts, food, chili cookoff, parade. Little Miss and Mister Yorktown Contest, cloggers, shoot-outs, grand parade, volleyball tourney, triple crown cookoff. (512) 564-2661.

II

Annual Events

Be sure to check local newspapers for specific dates of festivals and other activities. Most are annual events but the dates vary from year to year. Some events are not listed, such as plays and other productions presented frequently at Victoria College, Corpus Christi State University, and the Harbor Playhouse. Check local listings for these quality performances. Look under the city descriptors for a more detailed explanation of the events listed.

January:

Corpus Christi:

Corpus Christi Boat Show — (512) 991-0369
Gulf Coast Antique Show — (512) 682-6403
Boar's Head and Yule Log Festival — (512) 854-3044
Waterfront Art Market — (512) 880-3474
R.V. Show — (713) 589-7991
Nueces County Jr. Livestock Show — (512) 387-5395
County Jr. Livestock Show & Parade — (512) 387-3933
Arts & Crafts Show — (512) 991-2438
Corpus Christi Symphony — (512) 882-4091
First Friday Uptown Arts Event — (512) 883-7777
New Year's Day 2-mile Swim — (512) 880-3460

Rose Show — (512) 884-5264
Kingsville:
    Martin Luther King, Jr. Day Parade — (512) 592-6516

February:

Corpus Christi:
    A.A.U.W. Book Sale — (512) 991-2999
    South Texas Doll & Toy Show — (512) 991-2999
    Winterfest Travel Show — (512) 528-2597
    Trail Ride to San Antonio
    Valentine's 2,000 Meter Swim — (512) 880-5858
    Auto Show — (512) 880-5858
    The Corpus Christi Kantorei — (512) 994-2335
    Texas Leisure Sports Expo — (512) 991-2999
    Valentine's Day Arts & Crafts Show — (512) 991-2236
    Custom Car & Hot Rod Show — (512) 887-0009
    Winterfest — (512) 528-2597
    Arts & Crafts — (512) 991-2438
Goliad:
    U.S. Air Force Band of the West Concert — (512)
      645-2666
Kingsville:
    Annual Children's Show — (512) 595-3901
Port Aransas:
    Black & Red Ball — (512) 749-5919
    Rotary Club Spaghetti Dinner — (512) 749-5919
Schroeder:
    Trail Ride: To San Antonio Live Stock Show
Yorktown:
    Stock Show

March:

Corpus Christi:
    Gulf Coast Gem & Mineral Show — (512) 883-8543
    Air Force Band Concert — (512) 884-2011
    Annual African Violet Show — (512) 992-4571
    Irish Parade — (512) 888-3218
    Gun Show — (512) 663-3218
    Folklife Festival — (512) 883-0639
    C.C. 5,000 Meter Swim — (512) 852-0243

Birds & Flowers Tour — (512) 993-9885
Easter Egg Hunt
Arts & Crafts Show — (512) 991-2438
Falfurrias:
Falfurrias Funfest — (512) 325-3333
Four Seasons Bazaar — (512) 325-2918
Goliad:
La Bahia Downs Horse Races — (512) 645-8208
Goliad County Fair & Rodeo — (512) 645-3563
Fannin Memorial Service — (512) 645-3563
Kingsville:
Jazz Festival — (512) 595-2803
Kleberg/Kenedy County Fair & Stock Show — (512) 592-5229
Music Club Competition — (512) 592-2374
Texas A&I Rodeo — (512) 595-3713
Coastal Bend Regional History Fair — (512) 595-2810
Port Aransas:
Wild Game & Seafood Dinner — 1-800-242-3084
Port Lavaca:
Annual Seafood Opener Golf Tournament
Portland:
Pioneer Days — (512) 643-2475
Rockport/Fulton:
Oysterfest — (512) 729-7529
Victoria:
PRCA Rodeo — (512) 573-5141
Jaycees Stock Show (512) 575-0633
Women's Clubhouse Spring Bazaar — (512) 573-4441
Wild West Revue Arts & Crafts Show — (512) 576-1291
Games Party — (512) 575-8524
Invitation to the Dance — (512) 576-4500
Arts & Crafts Show — (512) 574-5378

April:

Corpus Christi:
Buccaneer Days — (512) 882-3242
Arts & Crafts Show — (512) 991-2438
Kingsville:
South Texas Spring Festival — (512) 595-3986

Blue Angels Air Show — (512) 595-6146
Fashion Show & Dinner
Arts & Crafts Show
Automobile, Boats & Farm Equipment Show
Battle of Country/Western Bands
Taste of Klegerg County
Student Carnival
Area Tour — J. E. Connor Museum, Horse Center, Henrietta Memorial Museum, Seller's Market, Naval Air Station, King Ranch
International Style Show
Carnival
International Student Bazaar
South Texas Pinto Bean Cookoff
Spring Formal Dance
Battle of Popular Bands & Dance
Festival of Christian Music
Wild Game Feast

Port Lavaca:
Spring Art Show
Port O'Connor:
Matagorda Island Adventure — (512) 983-2898
Seadrift:
Annual Oyster Shucking Contest
Victoria:
Fine Arts Festival — (512) 578-6555
Hello Follies — (512) 572-0931
Jazz it up Home & Energy Show (512) 576-1291
Arts & Crafts Show — (512) 578-0508

May:

Alice:
Festival Bandana
Corpus Christi:
Buccaneer Days — (512) 882-3242
Ultimate Yacht Race
Fiesta Botanica Weekend — (512) 993-7551
Texas Weapon Collector's Gun Show — (512) 663-3218
Naval Air Show & Open House — (512) 939-2674
U.S. Sailboard Open — (512) 884-2011

Art Association of Corpus Christi Exhibit — (512) 994-0774

Olympic Regatta — (512) 884-5892

Arts & Crafts Show — (512) 991-2438

Beach to Bay Marathon — (512) 993-5838

Falfurrias:

Fiesta Ranchera — (512) 325-3333

Port Aransas:

A Taste of Port Aransas — (512) 749-5131

Port Lavaca:

Cinco de Mayo

Seafood Golf Tournament

Port O'Connor:

Memorial Day Fishing Tournament — (512) 983-2671

Victoria:

Arts & Crafts Show — (512) 578-0508

County Arts & Crafts Fair — (512) 576-1291

South Texas Farm & Ranch Show — (512) 575-4581

Symphonic Showpieces — (512) 576-4500

Coin Show — (512) 575-0259

Paperback Book Sale — (512) 578-5329

June:

Alice:

Youth Rodeo — (512) 664-0401

Corpus Christi:

Texas State Stamp Show

Sunday Night Band Concert — (512) 880-3460

C.C. Beach Party — (512) 880-3460

Melodrama — (512) 882-3356

Planetarium — (512) 992-0130

C-Sculpture — (512) 289-1000

Falfurrias:

Watermelon Festival — (512) 325-5621

Falfurrias Mexican Village — (512) 325-5621

Goliad:

Longhorn Stampede — (512) 645-3563

Galvez Fiesta & Spanish Nightwatch — (512) 645-3752

Kingsville:

George Strait Team Roping — (512) 592-8516

Juneteenth Celebration — (512) 595-6438
Padre Island:
    C-Sculpture — (512) 289-1000
Port Aransas:
    Petticoat Fishing Tourney — (512) 749-5880
    National Championship of Port Aransas Bay Fishing
        Tourney — (512) 749-5252
    Gulf Coast Conservation Association Fishing Tourney
        (512) 749-5252
    Masters' Fishing Tourney — (512) 749-5880
    Texas Championship Billfish Tourney — (512) 882-4384
Port Lavaca:
    Calhoun County Youth Rodeo
    Juneteenth
Seadrift:
    Texas Water Safari Race
Sinton:
    TYRA Youth Rodeo — (512) 364-3641
Victoria:
    Antique Car Show — (512) 576-1291
    Beach Festival — (512) 578-1297
    Country Arts & Crafts Fair — (512) 576-1291
    PRCA Rodeo — (512) 573-5141

July:

Alice:
    Menudo Cookoff — (512) 664-0931
Aransas Pass:
    Blessing of the Fleet
Corpus Christi:
    Texas Jazz Festival — (512) 854-9634
    Creative Arts Center ART/CAMP (512) 888-5692
    Grayfest — (512) 528-2597
    Hunting and Fishing Show — (713) 589-7991
    Melodrama (512) 882-3356
    Planetarium (512) 992-0130
Falfurrias:
    Rodeo — Fourth of July
Goliad:
    LaBahia Downs Horse Races — (512) 645-8208

pork ribs. It is not true that Texans barbeque everything except lettuce, although they have been accused of it. South Texans are even picky about which wood they use when barbequeing. Mesquite wood is the current choice. All cooks in this area have their very own specialized BBQ sauce recipe. While the meat is cooking ever so slowly, one must be sure to baste the meat thoroughly and often with this spicy sauce. If the desired result is achieved, a knife is never needed to cut it. Side dishes of BBQ are jalapeno peppers, cole slaw, baked beans, potato salad, raw onions, pickles, and a side dish of extra sauce. Sissies use paper plates and utensils. Real Texans use butcher paper or brown wrapping paper.

BBQ SAUCE (VERY BASIC)

1 cup wine vinegar
1 cup vegetable oil
Small can of tomato paste

Salt, pepper, garlic powder, ground cumin to taste

MEXICAN FOOD:

The difference between true Mexican food and Tex-Mex is that one is light and more subtle while Tex-Mex is heavier, greasier, very filling, and delicious. A genuine Tex-Mex dinner consists of chili, tortilla chips, nachos (tortilla chips layered with melted cheddar cheese and jalapeno peppers), refried beans, rice, tamales, tacos, enchiladas, steamed soft tortillas, guacamole salad (avocado), chili con queso, and a dessert of pralines.

Chili — The National Dish of Texas:

Chili began in San Antonio. In the 1880s chili "queens" sold their chili from carts in the town square until health officials closed them down in the 1940s. It contained only meat and peppers simmered into a stewlike dish. Today it contains tomatoes and is also referred to as "bowl of fire" and "bowl of red." True chili is spicy, meaty, tasty, and most of all, HOT! It is acceptable to put crumbled crackers or tortilla chips in one's chili. Sour cream or cheddar cheese are modern day ad-

147

ditives. Coarsely ground beef is suitable for making chili, but many South Texans use ground venison instead and true Texans prefer it. When eating chili, do not become alarmed if sweat breaks out on your brow, your eyes water, or your sinus cavities open. This is a normal reaction.

ROGER'S CHILI

1–1¹/₂ lbs. ground venison or beef
1 large can tomato sauce
1 large can stewed tomatoes, diced
2 cans pinto beans
2 tbsp. cornstarch
1 bean can of water
2–4 tbsp. chili powder
¹/₂ stick margarine
1 onion
1 large jalapeno

In a large deep skillet or casserole dish brown meat with diced onion. When meat is browned stir in chili to taste — add tomato sauce, tomatoes, and beans. Stir in and simmer — mix cornstarch with water and stir in covered pot and simmer ¹/₂ hour to an hour. The longer it simmers, the better it gets).

A GUIDE TO WHAT YOU ARE EATING:

Burrito — Flour tortilla folded around spicy beef, covered (or filled) with chili, cheese, and onions.

Chili — a spicy stewlike dish containing tomatoes, peppers, and meat.

Chili con queso — a flat tortilla covered with melted cheese.

Chile rellenos — large peppers stuffed with spicy meat, cheese, and raisin mixture.

Enchilada — steamed, soft tortilla filled with refried beans, beef, or chicken, covered with chili and cheese and onions and rolled up.

Flautas — Tightly rolled tortillas, stuffed with spicy beef or chicken filling, that are deep-fat fried.

Frijoles — beans (pintos) cooked with water, salt pork, and onions.

Frijoles refritos — refried beans — cooked beans fried in lard and mashed until they resemble mashed potatoes.

Guacamole — ripe avocados mashed into a salad with tomatoes, chiles, and chopped onions; great topping for tacos, tostadas, or nachos.

Huevos — eggs.

Huevos rancheros — eggs covered with tomatoes, onions and peppers; big breakfast favorite.

Nachos — tortilla chips covered with refried beans and cheese, and dotted with slices of jalapeno pepper.

Pollo — chicken — shredded into enchiladas or topping for tostadas and tacos.

Salsa cruda — the most important thing on the table — spicy, hot red-colored sauce made from chopped chiles, cilantro, garlic, onions, and tomatoes. Habit forming. Great to dip chips into or add to other dishes.

Taco — a tortilla folded in the middle and deep-fat fried into a U-shape; filled with ground, spicy meat; topped with shredded iceberg lettuce and fresh chopped tomatoes, sour cream, cheese and salsa cruda.

Tacos al carbon — thin strips of charcoal-grilled beef wrapped in a soft tortilla.

Tamale — masa harina (corn meal pudding) beaten with lard, and smeared on a corn husk; filled with a spicy meat, rolled up and steamed. Remove husk before eating!

Tortilla — thin pancake of ground dried maize or masa harina deep fried or steamed.

Tostada — fried tortilla covered with refried beans, shredded lettuce, chicken or beef, cheese, onions, and guacamole.

Manzanilla tea — the Mexican version of camomile tea.

CHICKEN FRIED STEAK

Chicken Fried Steak or CFS is a main staple of South Texans. A weekly serving is necessary to ensure proper growth and balance. It comes in many shapes and forms but always involves pan fried steak that has been rolled in a flour mixture. A white gravy is served with authentic CFS. The gravy is served over homemade biscuits, not rice.

MEDIUM WHITE SAUCE

**2 tbsp. butter or bacon
grease
2 tbsp. all-purpose flour**

**¹/₄ tsp. salt
1 cup milk
3 dashes of black pepper**

Melt butter or heat bacon grease in saucepan over low heat. Blend in flour, salt, and black pepper. Add milk all at once. Cook quickly, stirring constantly, till mixture thickens and bubbles.

"NICE EATIN' "

We have refrained from giving our opinions of these establishments and trust you to be your own judge. We will say that one of us or a member of our family has eaten at most of these restaurants and had very good luck!

Alice:
Chanters Mexican Restaurant — 107 Cecilia — (512) 668-9781
Wayne's — Falfurrias Hwy. — (512) 664-7329

Aransas Pass:
The Bakery Cafe — 434 S. Commercial — (512) 758-3511

Bayside:
Crofutt's Bakery & Sandwich Shop — FM Rd. 136 — (512) 529-6663

Beeville:
Shorty's Place — 702 S. Washington — (512) 358-7302

Berclair:
Moya's — (512) 439-7249

Corpus Christi:
B&J Pizza — 6335 S.P.I.D. — (512) 992-6671
Bamboo Garden — 1220 Airline Rd. — (512) 993-7993
Bar-B-Q Man — 4931 Interstate Hwy. 37 South
The Black-eyed Pea — 4801 S.P.I.D. — (512) 993-4588.
Cajun Reef — 1002 N. Chaparral — (512) 883-5123

Capers — In the Marriot on Shoreline Dr. — 707 N. Shoreline Blvd. — (512) 882-1700

Che Bello's — 320-C William St. (In the Totally Texas Courts) — (512) 882-8832

County Line — 6102 Ocean Drive — (512) 991-7427

Crystal's Confectionary — Parkdale Plaza — (512) 857-8081

Elmo's — 6335 S. Staples — (512) 992-3474

Elmo's Road House Inn — 622 N. Water — (512) 883-1643

Executive Surf Club — 309 N. Water — (512) 884-7873

Frank's Spaghetti House — 2724 Leopard — (512) 882-0075

Friday's P.O.E.T.S. — 4825 Saratoga Blvd. — (512) 991-4574, 555 N. Carancahua — 882-7638

Landry's — 600 N. Shoreline, People's Street T-Head — (512) 882-6666.

La Parisienne — 42 Lamar Park Shopping Center — (512) 857-2736

Lighthouse Restaurant & Oyster Bar — Lawrence Street T-Head — (512) 883-3982

Luciano's — 1618 S. Staples — (512) 884-1832

Mao-Tai Chinese Restaurant — 4601 S. Padre Island Dr. — (512) 852-8877

Memo's Mexican Food Restaurant — 5884 Everhart — (512) 992-4562

Old Mexico Restaurant — 3329 Leopard — (512) 883-6461

Olive Garden Italian Restaurant — 5258 S. Padre Island Drive — (512) 992-4742

Origami — Sushi Bar — Airline and McArdle — (512) 993-3966

Reflections Marriott — 900 N. Shoreline — (512) 886-3515

Rusty's Gourmet Hamburgers — 1645 Airline — (512) 993-5000

Snoopy's Pier — 13313 S. Padre Island Drive — (512) 949-8815

Taqueria Jalisco — No. 1 — 902 S. Port Ave. — (512) 881-8739

Taqueria Jalisco — No. 2 — 2341 Horne Rd. — (512) 855-1162

Taqueria Jalisco — No. 3 — 9729 S. Padre Island Dr. —
(512) 937-4606

Wallbanger's — 4102 S. Staples — (512) 855-8007

 Water Street Oyster Bar — 309 N. Water — (512)
881-9448

Yardarm Restaurant — 4310 Ocean Dr. — (512) 855-8157

Goliad:

La Bahia — Refugio Hwy. — (512) 645-3651

Kenedy:

Barth's — 445 N. Sunset Street — (512) 583-2468

Church's — 110 N. Sunset Strip — (512) 583-9030

Kenedy's Finest — 106 S. Sunset Strip — (512) 583-3262

Shorty's Steak House — 13 miles north of Kenedy

Kingsville:

Sirloin Stockade — 1500 Brahma Blvd. — (512) 595-1182

Seller's Market — 205 E. Kleberg — (512) 595-4992

Oakville:

Van's Bar-B-Que — (512) 786-3995

Port Aransas:

Pelican's Landing — 116 W. Roberts — (512) 749-6405

Purple Parrot — Port Royal on Mustang Island — (512)
749-5011

Quarter Deck — 914 Tarpon — (512) 749-4449

Seafood & Spaghetti Works — 710 S. Alister — (512)
749-4333

Tortuga Flats — 821 Trout — (512) 749-4333

Port Lavaca:

The Crow's Nest — Magnolia Beach — (512) 552-1964

El Patio Cafe — 534 W. Main — (512) 552-6316

Ocean Inn — 116 N. Commerce — (512) 552-7650

Port O'Connor:

The Beachcomber — Maple St. — (512) 983-2992

Josie's Mexican Food — Adams St. — (512) 983-4720

Portland:

Mac's Bar-B-Que — 219 Hwy. 35 — (512) 643-5589

Marco's — Hwy. 181 — (512) 643-7919

Refugio:

Moya's Mexican Food — 401 2nd — (512) 526-9124

Slasher's Bar-B-Que — 511 N. Alamo St. — (512) 526-5554

Two Jim's — 901 Bayou — (512) 526-2579

Riviera:

King's Inn — (512) 297-5265

Robstown:

Cotten's Bar-B-Que — Hwy. 77 — (512) 767-9973

Don Manuel's — 432 W. Main Ave. — (512) 387-4595

Rockport:

Charlotte Plummer's — Fulton Beach Road — (512) 729-1185

Copano Provisioning Company — Hwy. 35 N at Holiday Beach — (512) 729-1703

Key Allegro Marina — 37 Mazatlan — (512) 729-2761

Sinton:

Back Street Cafe — 293 Rachel — (512) 364-2445

Chat and Chew — (512) 364-1512

Jim's Country Inn — 1101 E. Sinton — (512) 364-4995

Odem's Bar-B-Que — Hwy. 77 between Sinton and Odem — (512) 364-4485

Skidmore:

Chisholm Trail Bar-B-Que — Hwy. 181 N — (512) 287-3847

Taft:

Mary's — 518 Davis Rd. — (512) 528-3612

Victoria:

Fossati's Deli — 302 S. Main — (512) 578-3354

Leo's Chuckwagon — 1411 Port Lavaca — (512) 578-9381

Marco's — 7702 N. Navarro — (512) 576-9961

Old Victoria — 207 N. Navarro — (512) 572-8841

Woodsboro:

Wilson's Railway Station — 10 Wood Ave. — (512) 543-4900

DAY TRIPS:

Go on a Border Binge!

Turn south and head for the Rio Grande River, the only thing that divides Texas and Mexico. Local yokels go frequently. The Coastal Bend Area is a mere hop, skip, and a jump from three popular border towns. While not totally Mexican, they still offer a great experience where you can spend a little bit of money on a whole lot of fun. Half the fun is bartering with the shopkeepers and it doesn't hurt to know a bit of Spanish. In the market be sure to check out the pottery, Mexican dresses, vanilla, paper flowers, tortilla accessories, pinatas, lace tablecloths and serapes. (Be sure to avoid the jumping beans, sequined sombreros, and oil paintings on black velvet.)

From Corpus Christi:

Matamoros — 160 miles — Across from Brownsville. One of Mexico's wealthy cotton centers. Lovely woven goods are available in the markets *(mercados)*. The Fiesta Internacional is celebrated with Brownsville in September, honoring Mexican independence. Frog legs are best at Arturo's.

Reynosa — 152 miles — Across from McAllen. This quiet, captivating town has much to offer: *mercados,* Sunday afternoon bullfights, and of course, Sam's. A great game dinner is yours to be had only two blocks from Mexican customs. Its motif is a hunting lodge. During whitewing season, prepare to wait a bit. The International Museum is shared by Reynosa and McAllen. It contains historical memorabilia from the United States and Mexico. Also arts and crafts.

Nuevo Laredo — 144 miles — Across from Laredo. Accessible by Highway 59 South. Local *mercados* have a splendid selection of Mexican jewelry and precious metalworks. Surprisingly, one of the most exciting celebrations each year is a four-day event honoring George Washington as the first Western Hemisphere leader to free the New World from Old World dominance. Shoppers must visit Marti's to view clothing for the entire family. "Victoria's" is a restaurant three blocks off the bridge with excellent food, and set in the historic Longoria home.

MORE DAY TRIPS!

San Antonio — Two hours and fifteen minutes away, spend a day or a week. Actually, it is 145 miles from Corpus Christi to San Antonio, but in Texas, that is less than a mere morning away (Note: South Texans do not measure distance in miles but in the number of hours it takes to get there). This place has a little bit of everything. The wonderful river walk, beautiful historic sights all over town such as the Alamo, Arneson River Theatre, La Villita Settlement, Spanish Governor's Palace, Institute of Texan Cultures, Buckhorn Hall of Horns, Mission Trail (4 Missions), Witte Museum, McNay Art Institute, San Antonio Zoo, Japanese Tea Garden and King William District, a lovely street of mansions originally settled by German merchants in the late 19th century. We mustn't forget to mention Hemisfair Plaza with 750-foot Tower of the Americas. It offers 2 sky-high dining levels plus observation deck with beautiful views of Alamo City, and of course Sea World, which is worth the trip itself. Wonderful restaurants, great shopping malls, and good lodging add to the fun of San Antonio.

The Valley — Consider a day trip to the Brownsville, McAllen, Harlingen area for a variety of reasons such as the Gladys Porter Zoo, Mexico, or stock up on Valley citrus.

Laguna Atascosa — Wildlife refuge outside Harlingen and Santa Anna Wildlife Refuge outside McAllen on the Rio Grande.

South Padre Island — for more beaches, excellent restaurants, shopping, and fishing.

LOOKIN' PURTY:

If you want to look like a native of South Texas, you must start from the boots up! You can get outfitted for these at the Running W Saddle Shop in Kingsville, Wilson's Western Wear in Portland, Beeville, Corpus Christi and Woodsboro, and Saenz Western Wear in Beeville. Next, you'll need Levi's (tight), a belt with a big, flashy buckle, and a plaid western shirt. Monogrammed khaki shirts are also acceptable. Real men don't wear bandanas but all their women do. They usually have several in assorted colors. Red, black, and white is best, of course. Used as a scarf, belt, sweat-band, decorated with beads, rhinestones, and studs, they prefer them as sparkly as possible. Texas women love to wear jewelry. Top off your outfit with the second most important statement next to the boots — the western hat. Many different styles and creases are acceptable. Not only is the western look fun — it's durable, comfortable, and practical.

Men can also fit in with guayaberas, the traditional Mexican wedding shirt. These shirts are large, airy, and comfortable in the heat. They are also sharp and crisp looking with elaborate embroidery on the front.

SAY IT RYTE (RIGHT):

It is futile to attempt to correct the speech of South Texans. If you do so they will patiently explain to you that they do not speak funny or different; the rest of the world does. If you want to "fit in" keep these articulation and pronunciation rules in mind:

aigs — eggs
athalete — athlete
awl — oil
ax — ask
big dill — big deal
bizness — business
dija — did you ("dija" see her hat?)
far — fire
flire — flour
gin-yu-wine — genuine
hep — help
ire — our (come on over to "ire" house, y'all hear?)
fixinto — South Texans are never "about" to do anything. They are "fixinto bake a cake" or "fixinto go to town."
tallit — toilet
thang — thing
y'all — synonomous with Northern "you's" guys. It is the plural form of you all. Has been known to be taught in some primary grades as a true contraction as if you all is correct. (Isn't it?)

156

WINTER TEXANS — SNOW BIRDS:

Definition — a "snow bird" is a winter visitor from anywhere north or east of the Texas state line. He resides in South Texas most of the winter and is delighted to be away from the harsh winters "back home." Their motto is "If you don't like Texas weather — stick around — it'll change in a day or two!" How to recognize — drives anything from a camper truck to a big-bucks RV (Recreational Vehicle). Wears deck shoes, casual clothes, and almost nothing western. Appearance is clean-cut and neat.

How he spends his money — They are welcome patrons of grocery stores, R.V. Parks, and local gift shops for those little souvenirs they like to take home to the kids and grandchildren — or a remembrance of their visit to the coast. What they prefer to be called — Winter Texans.

His Haunts — Rockport is understandably a favorite. Are happy in any coastal fishing village like Port Lavaca, Port Aransas, and Aransas Pass. His attitude — excellent. Smiles politely at South Texans' mutilation of the King's English. Doesn't poke fun at "real" Texans too often or too much. Tolerates snow bird jokes quite well. Some of the best volunteers available for those special projects they're interested in. A credit to any community they inhabit.

SPRING BREAKERS:

Definition — a "spring breaker" is a visitor that resides primarily at any university campus. Their migration occurs during March and April for one to two week durations. The migration is fueled in part by a search of the first "rays" of springtime sun.

How to recognize — drives any vehicle with writing on the windows. Wears the most current of trendy tee shirts, the brightest shorts, the biggest sunglasses and otherwise almost nothing at all. Skin color ranges from lily white to lobster red.

How he spends his money — party beverages, party food, party clothes, party rooms, party sun lotion. His motto — "Let's Padre!" His haunts — the beach, the beach restaurants, the beach condos, the beach motels, the beach stores. His attitude — wild and crazy guys — Let's Padre!

(Avoid the Port Aransas ferry during these migrations.)

SENTIMENTAL JOURNEY:

One can learn a great deal about an area from a quiet visit to a local cemetery. Today, most folks only go to cemeteries when a loved one dies. They usually hold only sad feelings for all of us, but that wasn't always so. Not long ago, families regularly visited the graves of their departed loved ones. Cemeteries were often adjacent to the families' places of worship and it was a common happening to see the resting places of one's relatives on a regular basis. Families spent time there caring for the grounds around their family's tombstones, recalling good times and bad.

As you visit a town's cemeteries you can pick up attitudes and values of the people who lived and died there. In the Live Oak Cemetery on Lamar Peninsula north of Rockport, this cryptic verse speaks to us from a stone,

> Stop here, and look as you pass by,
> Where you are now, so once was I,
> Where I am now, so once you'll be,
> Prepare for death and follow me!

In an obscure little cemetery near Yorktown, hidden beneath brush and trees, we found this sweet little verse from someone sorely missed,

> 'Tis hard to break
> the tender cord
> When love has bound the heart.
> 'Tis hard, so hard
> to speak the words
> We must forever part.

158

The oldest burial place in South Texas is the old San Patricio cemetery in San Patricio which is west of Calallen. It lies very near the old San Patricio Church. There are many Irish names there as well as Spanish names. It was interesting to note that unlike some cemeteries, there were no ethnic boundaries here. People from different countries, as well as different heritages, were laid to rest side by side, which speaks commendably about the community and how well they got along with one another. Some beautiful rubbings were taken from this place as well as this farewell,

No pain, no grief, no anxious fear,
Can reach our loved one sleeping here

The art of gravestone rubbing is ancient, inexpensive, and easy. You may purchase fine quality paper, which is lovely for framing, or butcher paper until you get the hang of it. A hard ball rubbing pigment or large crayon is needed. Tape your paper to the stone you want to rub. Then place a good bit of pressure on the crayon and rub back and forth until you see the pattern you wish to save. These look lovely matted and framed.

IV

Antiques

On the Antique Trail:

The following is a list of some of the antique stores of the Coastal Bend area.

Aransas Pass:

Daniel's Den Antiques — 315 E. Wilson, Aransas Pass, TX 78336. Primitives, American and European antiques. Jeanne Baen, 547-2173.

Corpus Christi:

A to Z Auctions — 3305 Ayers, (512) 888-6445.

Antique Finders, Inc. — 1037 Airline, Corpus Christi, TX 78412. Antique furniture, glass, primitives, dolls (new & old). Mon.–Sat. 10–5, Alva Blaine. 991-2040.

Antique Treasures — 5412 Everhart, (512) 993-6682.

Antiquity — 319 N. Chaparral, (512) 882-2424.

Attic Antiques — P.O. Box 2592, Corpus Christi, TX 78403. Sterling matching. Service, appraisals. "See us at all the finer antique shows." 991-2733.

Betty Gresham Antiques & Appraisals — 10901 Leopard, Corpus Christi, TX 78410. Member of ISA. Personal property, insurance and estates, china, glass, Oriental porcelain, furniture, Bric-a-Brac, estate sales. Mon–Sat, 9:30–5, 241-7062.

Brown's Collectables — 1010 Santa Fe, 882-2424.

The Carousel — 4820-A Kostoryz, (512) 885-8563.

Carry-Lo Antique Shoppe — 1205 McKenzie, (512) 881-8220.

The Castor Collection — 38 Lamar Park Center, (512) 881-8052.

Collectors World — 1214 Rickey, (512) 991-9812.

Consignment World — Sunrise Mall, (512) 991-7733.

Country Peddlers — 4337 S. Alameda, (512) 993-7237.

Country Peddler's Downtown — 317 N. Chaparral, (512) 887-6618.

Deja Vu — 4206 Avalon, (512) 991-8678.

Dickson W. E. Co. — 4220 S. Padre Island Dr. (512) 857-0063.

E.O. Antiques and Cabinets — 1811–21 Ayers, Corpus Christi, TX 78404. Interior design, art glass, cut glass, lamps, paintings and fine furniture. James Elliot & A. T. Ogg. Mon–Sat, 9–6, 888-5442, 882-8212.

Ettleman's Discontinued China & Crystal Service — P.O. Box 6491, Corpus Christi, TX 78411. China: Caselton, Flintridge, Franciscan, Haviland, Lenox, Oxford & Syracuse. Crystal: Cambridge, Duncan, Fostoria, Lenox & Tiffiny. 888-8391.

The Family Attic — 602 Naval Air Station, (512) 939-7320.

Fullilove Antiques & Interiors — 1233 S. Staples, (512) 884-9111.

Gardner W. Ltd. — 1524 S. Staples, (512) 887-4553.

Gene's Antiques — 4331 S. Alameda, Corpus Christi, TX 78412. Selective variety, American, Victorian, and Country furniture, sterling matching, art, cut and depression glass, china, quilts, lamps, dolls, clocks. Mon–Sat 10–6, H. E. (Gene) Haralson, 994-0440.

Golden Antiques — 1105 S. Staples, Corpus Christi, TX 78404, between Craig & Buford. Old glass, china, brass, silver, collectibles and many beautiful fine pieces of American and European furniture. Closed Fri. & Sun., Sylvia Golden Dean, 884-0442.

Good Company — 1010 Santa Fe, (512) 888-9160.

Betty Gresham Antiques & Appraisals — 10901 Leopard, Corpus Christi, TX 78410. Member of ISA. Personal property, insurance and estates, china, glass, Oriental porcelain, furniture, Bric-a-Brac, estate sales. Mon–Sat, 9:30–5, 241-7062.

Hobbit-Hole, 422 Sam Rankin, (512) 882-8455.

Home Sweet Home Antique Market — 4333 S. Alameda, Corpus Christi, TX 78412. Over 20 dealers, antiques, art, crafts, gifts, refinishing, etc. Lynn Lawrence, 991-4001.

Lee-Cunningham, Inc., Interior Designers — 3100 S. Alameda, Corpus Christi, TX 78412. English and European imports, Oriental pieces of merit from the late 18th & 19th centuries. Mon.–Fri., 8:30–5, 882-4482.

Libbie's Antiques & Crafts — 5566 Ayers, (512) 855-6231.

Moore Clay Auctions & Appraisals — 1601 Mesquite, (512) 883-7745.

Murphy's — 4610 Kostoryz, (512) 854-2508.

Odds & Ends — 9841 S. Padre Island Dr., (512) 937-8944.

The Pumpkin Patch — 4333 Kostoryz, (512) 855-5425.

Quaint Shop — 811 S. Staples, Corpus Christi, TX 78404. Country and Victorian furniture, primitives, folk art, candles, stuffed animals, sinfully delicious custom designed cakes, paperback book exchange, VISA, Mastercard, Layaways. Tues.–Sat., 10–5, Melissa Lemmon, 844-9541.

Remarkable Consignments — Furniture and bric-a-brac. All consignment items from the finest homes in the Coastal Bend Area. 3636 S. Alameda. Mon.–Sat., (512) 851-8353.

Rosie's Antique Shop — 4832 S. Alameda, (512) 852-2323.

Second Hand Rose — 4343 S. Alameda, Corpus Christi, TX 78404. Off the wall, offbeat filled with dolls, teddy bears, vintage clothing, costume jewelry, gift items, stuffed animals, etc. All displayed in and on a few antiques. Mon–Sat, 11–5, Helen Williams, 882-5608.

Sister Sue's — 4343 S. Alameda, (512) 992-5300.

Six Points Antiques — 1612 S. Staples, Corpus Christi, TX 78404. Primitives, toys, dolls, glass & sewing machines, Mon.–Fr., 9:30–5, Sat. till 12, C. E. Calhoun, 888-6184.

Today's Treasures, 4820 Kostoryz — (512) 853-7405.

Two J's Consignments & Antiques — 522 Everhart, (512) 857-7736.

Unique Antiques — 4803 S. Alameda, (512) 993-0762.

The Wild Goose Chase — 3509 S. Staples, (512) 851-9533.

George West:

Rosie's Treasures — Main, (512) 449-2950.

Goliad:

The Honeycomb — 100 N. Courthouse Square, (512) 645-2331.

Odem:

Bain's Junk & Jewels — Highway 77, (512) 368-2066.

Port Lavaca:

A Little Bit Country — Highway 35 South, (512) 552-6616.

Joyce Shilling's Antiques — 1000 Purple Sage, (512) 552-3059.

Refugio:

The White House — 1108 Power St., (512) 526-4507.

Robstown:

The Catch All — FM Rd. 624, (512) 387-6258.

Past & Present — Industrial Blvd. (512) 387-2686.

Trash & Treasures — 201 N. 5th, Robstown, (512) 387-2686.

Rockport:

Bent Tree Galleries — 504 S. Austin, (512) 729-4822.

Este Maude's Haus — N. Hwy, 35, (512) 729-1924.

Harcrow's Bluebonnett Mall — FM 1069, (512) 729-1724.

Maritime Gallery — 701 Allen, (512) 729-7873.

Mary Ann's Antiques — 1005 Main (512) 729-1945.

Orleans House — 1320 Orleans (512) 729-3601.

This That & The Other — 312 S. Bronte, (512) 729-7934.

Yardley Imports — 1500 Rant, (512) 729-8816.

Sinton:

Gwen's Antiques — Highway 181, (512) 364-1165.

Three Rivers:

Town & Country Antiques, Highway 281, (512) 786-4822.

Victoria:

Antiques R Us — Victoria Mall, (512) 575-8586.

Christy Donoghue Antiques, Inc. — 2424 N. Navarro, (512) 573-7895.

English Import Furniture — 1211 N. Laurent, (512) 565-6683.

Griffith's Antiques — 605 Larkspur, (512) 573-6467.

Mundine's Antiques & Collectibles — 607 E. Rio Grande (Houston Hwy.) (512) 576-9445.

R. P. Sales — 706 E. Red River, (512) 576-4984.

Scarboro Antiques — 503 E. Santa Rosa, (512) 576-5005.

Sister's — 206 W. Water St., (512) 575-5109.

Slotnick's Antiques and Collectibles — 108 N. Main, (512) 573-3423.

Victoria Antique Flea Market — 405 W. Water, (512) 578-3750.

Victoria Antique Shop — 804 Berkman Dr., (512) 575-2203.

The Way We Were — 401 Hathaway, (512) 578-0813.

V

Checklists

Bird Checklist:

Birds in the Coastal Bend frequent three main areas: the seashore, the lakes, and inland. We are blessed with a tremendously large and seasonal variety because we are in the middle of their migratory flyway! For your convenience, the lists are broken down in the three areas. The lists from the lakes and inland region were compiled by Gene Blacklock, Welder Wildlife Foundation. The seashore list was adapted from the Padre Island National Seashore list, naming only the more common species.

R = resident   S = summer   W = winter

The Seashore and Bays:

GREBES:
Pied-billed grebe — R

PELICANS AND CORMORANTS:
American White Pelican — R
Brown Pelican — R
Double-crested Cormorant — W
Olivaceous Cormorant — W
Magnificent Frigatebird — S

HERONS & BITTERNS:
Great Blue Heron — R
Great Egret — R
Snowy Egret — R
Little Blue Heron — R
Tri-colored Heron — R
Reddish Egret — R
Cattle Egret — R
Green-back Heron — R
Black-crown Night Heron — R
Yellow-crown N. Heron — R

IBIS, SPOONBILL:
White Ibis — R
White-faced Ibis — R
Roseate Spoonbill — R

SWAN, GEESE, DUCKS:
Greater White-fronted Goose — W
Snow Goose — W
Canada Goose — W
Green-winged Teal — W
Black Duck — W
Mottled Duck — R
Northern Pintail — W
Blue-winged Teal — W
Cinnamon Teal — W
Northern Shoveler — W
Gadwall — W
American Wigeon — W

Canvasback — W
Redhead — W
Greater Scaup — W
Bufflehead — W
Ruddy Duck — R

VULTURES, HAWKS, FALCONS:
Black Vulture — R
Turkey Vulture — R
Osprey — R
Mississippi Kite — S
Northern Harrier (Marsh Hawk) — R
Cooper's Hawk — R
American Kestrel — R
Peregrine Falcon — W

QUAIL, TURKEY:
Northern Bobwhite — R

RAILS, GALLINULES, COOT, CRANE:
Clapper Rail — R
King Rail — R
Purple Gallinule — R
Common Moorehen — R
American Coot — R
Sandhill Crane — W

SHOREBIRDS:
Black-bellied Plover — W
Snowy Plover — R
American Oystercatcher — R
Semipalmated Plover — W
Piping Plover — W
Killdeer — W
Black-necked Stilt — R
American Avocet — R
Greater Yellowlegs — W
Solitary Sandpiper — W
Willet — R
Spotted Sandpiper — W

165

Whimbrel — W
Long-billed Curlew — R
Marbled Godwit — W
Ruddy Turnstone — W
Red Knot — W
Sanderling — R
Semipalmated Sandpiper — W
Western Sandpiper — W
Least Sandpiper — W
Dunlin — W
Short-billed Dowitcher — W

GULLS AND TERNS:
Laughing Gull — R
Ring-billed Gull — W
Herring Gull — W
Gulf-billed Tern — R
Caspian Tern — R
Royal Tern — R
Sandwich Tern — R
Forster's Tern — R
Least Tern — R
Black Skimmer — R

PIGEONS AND DOVES:
Rock Dove — R
Mourning Dove — R
Inca Dove — R
Common Ground Dove — R
ANI:
Groove-billed Ani — R
OWLS AND GOATSUCKERS:
Common Nighthawk — R
SWIFTS, HUMMINGBIRDS,
   KINGFISHERS:
Belted Kingfisher — W
PERCHING BIRDS:
Scissor-tailed Flycatcher — S
Northern Mockingbird — R
Water Pipit — S
Common Yellowthroat — R
Seaside Sparrow — R
Swamp Sparrow — R
Red-winged Blackbird — R
Eastern Meadowlark — R
Western Meadowlark — R
Great-tailed Grackle — R
Brown-headed Cowbird — R
House Sparrow — R

Inland and Lakeside Birds:

GREBES:
Pied-Billed Grebe — R
Horned — N
Red-necked — W
Eared — W
PELICANS AND CORMORANTS:
American White Pelican — R
Brown Pelican — R
Double-crested Cormorant —
   W
Olivaceous Cormorant — W
ANHINGAS AND
   FRIGATEBIRDS:
Anhingas — R
Magnificent Frigatebird — S

HERONS AND IBISES:
American Bittern — W
Least Bittern — R
Great Blue Heron — R
Great Egret — R
Snowy Egret — R
Little Blue Heron — R
Reddish Egret — R
Tricolored Heron — R
Cattle Egret — R
Green-backed Heron — R
Black-crowned Night-Heron —
   R
Yellow-crowned Night-Heron
   — R

White Ibis — R
Glossy Ibis — S
White-faced Ibis — R
Roseate Spoonbill — R
Wood Stork — S
GEESE AND DUCKS:
Fulvous Whistling-Duck — S
Black-bellied Whistling-Duck — S
Tundra Swan — W
Greater White-fronted Goose — W
Snow Goose — W
Canada Goose — W
Wood Duck — R
Green-Winged Teal — W
American Black Duck — W
Mottled Duck — R
Mallard — W
Northern Pintail — W
Blue-winged Teal — W
Cinnamon Teal — W
Northern Shoveler — W
Gadwall — W
American Wigeon — W
Canvasback — W
Redhead — W
Ring-necked Duck — R
Greater Scaup — W
Lesser Scaup — W
Scoter — W
Common Goldeneye — W
Bufflehead Duck — W
Hooded Merganser — W
Common Merganser — W
Red-breasted Merganser — W
Ruddy Duck — W
Masked Duck — W
VULTURES AND HAWKS:
Black Vulture — R
Turkey Vulture — R
Osprey — R
American Swallow-tailed Kite — S

Black-shouldered Kite — S
Mississippi Kite — S
Bald Eagle — R
Northern Harrier — R
Sharp-shinned Hawk — W
Cooper's Hawk — R
Common Black Hawk — S
Harris's Hawk — R
Gray Hawk — S
Red-shouldered Hawk — R
Broad-winged Hawk — S
Swainson's Hawk — S
White-tailed Hawk — R
Red-tailed Hawk — R
Ferruginous Hawk — W
Rough-legged Hawk — W
Golden Eagle — W

CARACARAS AND FALCONS:
Crested Caracara — R
American Kestrel — W
Merlin — W
Peregrine Falcon — W
Prairie Falcon — W

TURKEYS AND QUAILS:
Plain Chachalaca — R
Wild Turkey — R
Northern Bobwhite Quail — R
Scaled Quail — R

RAILS AND CRANES:
Yellow Rail — W
Black Rail — W
Clapper Rail — R
King Rail — R
Virginia Rail — R
Sora — R
Purple Gallinule — R
Common Moorhen — R
American Coot — R
Sandhill Crane — W

167

PLOVERS, STILTS, SAND-
PIPERS, AND PHALAROPES:
Black-bellied Plover — W
Lesser Golden-Plover — S
Snowy Plover — R
Wilson's Plover — R
Semipalmated Plover — W
Piping Plover — W
Killdeer — W
American Oystercatcher — R
Black-necked Stilt — R
American Avocet — R
Northern Jacana — R
Greater Yellowlegs — W
Lesser Yellowlegs — W
Solitary Sandpiper — W
Spotted Sandpiper — W
Willet — R
Upland Sandpiper — W
Eskimo Curlew — W
Long-billed Curlew — R
Hudsonian Godwit — W
Marbled Godwit — W
Ruddy Turnstone — W
Red Knot — W
Sanderling — R
Semipalmated Sandpiper — W
Western Sandpiper — W
Least Sandpiper — W
White-rumped Sandpiper — W
Baird's Sandpiper — W
Pectoral Sandpiper — W
Dunlin — W
Stilt Sandpiper — W
Buff-breasted Sandpiper — S
Short-billed Dowitcher — W
Long-billed Dowitcher — W
Common Snipe — W
American Woodcock — W
Wilson's Phalarope — S
Red-necked Phalarope — S

GULLS AND TERNS:
Laughing Gull — R
Franklin's Gull — S
Bonaparte's Gull — W
Ring-billed Gull — W
Herring Gull — W
Gull-billed Tern — R
Caspian Tern — R
Royal Tern — R
Sandwich Tern — R
Common Tern — S
Forster's Tern — R
Least Tern — R
Black Tern — S
Blackkimmer — R

DOVES:
Rock Dove — R
White-winged Dove — R
Mourning Dove — R
Inca Dove — R
Common Ground-Dove — R

CUCKOOS:
Black-billed Cuckoo — S
Yellow-billed Cuckoo — S
Greater Roadrunner — R
Groove-billed Ani — R

OWLS AND NIGHTJAYS:
Common Barn-Owl — R
Eastern Screech-Owl — R
Great Horned Owl — R
Burrowing Owl — R
Barred Owl — R
Long-Eared Owl — W
Short-Eared Owl — W
Lesser Nighthawk — S
Common Nighthawk — R
Common Pauraque — R
Common Poorwill — S
Chuck-will's-widow — S
Whip-poor-will — W

SWIFTS AND HUMMINGBIRDS:
Chimney Swift — S
White-throated Swift — S
Buff-bellied Hummingbird — S
Ruby-throated Hummingbird — S
Black-chinned Hummingbird — S
Anna's Hummingbird — W
Broad-tailed Hummingbird — S
Rufous Hummingbird — S
Allen's Hummingbird — W

KINGFISHERS:
Ringed Kingfisher — S
Belted Kingfisher — R
Green Kingfisher — R

WOODPECKERS:
Red-bellied Woodpecker — R
Golden-fronted Woodpecker — R
Yellow-bellied Sapsucker — W
Ladder-backed Woodpecker — R
Downy Woodpecker — R
Hairy Woodpecker — R
Northern Flicker — W
Pileated Woodpecker — R

FLYCATCHERS:
Olive-sided Flycatcher — S
Western Wood-Pewee — S
Eastern Wood-Pewee — S
Yellow-bellied Flycatcher — S
Acadian Flycatcher — S
Alder Flycatcher — S
Willow Flycatcher — S
Least Flycatcher — S
Black Phoebe — R
Eastern Phoebe — W
Say's Phoebe — W
Vermillion Flycatcher — R
Ash-throated Flycatcher — S

Great Crested Flycatcher — S
Great Kiskadee — R
Couch's Kingbird — R
Cassin's Kingbird — S
Western Kingbird — S
Eastern Kingbird — S
Scissor-tailed Flycatcher — S

LARKS AND SWALLOWS:
Horned Lark — R
Purple Martin — S
Tree Swallow — R
Violet-green Swallow — S
Northern Rough-winged Swallow — R
Bank Swallow — S
Cliff Swallow — S
Barn Swallow — S

JAYS AND CROWS:
Blue Jay — W
Green Jay — R
American Crow — R
Chihuahuan Raven — R

CHICKADEE, TITMICE, AND VERDIN:
Carolina Chickadee — W
Tufted Titmouse — R
Verdin — R

NUTHATCHES AND CREEPERS:
Red-breasted Nuthatch — W
White-breasted Nuthatch — R
Brown Creeper — W

WRENS:
Cactus Wren — R
Carolina Wren — R
Bewick's Wren — R
House Wren — W
Winter Wren — W
Sedge Wren — W
Marsh Wren — W

KINGLETS AND
GNATCATCHERS:
Golden-crowned Kinglet — W
Ruby-crowned Kinglet — W
Blue-gray Gnatcatcher — R
THRUSHES, MOCKINGBIRDS,
AND THRASHERS:
Eastern Bluebird — R
Mountain Bluebird — W
Veery — S
Gray-cheeked Thrush — S
Swainson's Thrush — S
Hermit Thrush — W
Wood Thrush — S
American Robin — W
Gray Catbird — S
Northern Mockingbird — R
Sage Thrasher — W
Brown Thrasher — W
Long-billed Thrasher — W
Curve-billed Thrasher — R
PIPIT, WAXWINGS, AND
ALLIES:
Water Pipit — W
Sprague's Pipit — W
Cedar Waxwing — W
Phainopeola — R
SHRIKES AND STARLINGS:
Loggerhead Shrike — R
European Starling — W
VIREOS:
White-eyed Vireo — R
Bell's Vireo — S
Solitary Vireo — W
Yellow-throated Vireo — S
Warbling Vireo — S
Philadelphia Vireo — S
Red-eyed Vireo — S
WOOD WARBLERS:
Blue-winged Warbler — S
Golden-Tennessee Warbler — S
Tennessee Warbler — S

Orange-crowned Warbler — R
Nashville Warbler — R
Northern Parula — S
Yellow Warbler — S
Chestnut-sided Warbler — S
Magnolia Warbler — S
Black-throated Blue Warbler —
S
Yellow-rumped Warbler — S
Black-throated Gray Warbler
— S
Townsend's Warbler — S
Black-throated Green Warbler
— S
Golden-cheeked Warbler — S
Blackburnian Warbler — S
Yellow-throated Warbler — W
Pine Warbler — W
Prairie Warbler — S
Palm Warbler — W
Bay-breasted Warbler — S
Blackpoll Warbler — S
Cerulean Warbler — S
Black and White Warbler — S
American Redstart — S
Prothonotary Warbler — S
Worm-eating Warbler — S
Swainson's Warbler — S
Ovenbird — S
Northern Waterthrush — S
Louisiana Waterthrush — S
Kentucky Warbler — S
Connecticut Warbler — S
Mourning Warbler — S
MacGillivray's Warbler — S
Common Yellowthroat — R
Hooded Warbler — S
Wilson's Warbler — W
Canada Warbler — S
American Redstart — S
Yellow-breasted Chat — S

TANAGERS:
Hepatic Tanager — S
Summer Tanager — S
Scarlet Tanager — S
Western Tanager — S

GROSBEAKS, BUNTINGS, AND
  TOWHEES:
Northern Cardinal — R
Pyrrhuloxia — R
Rose-breasted Grosbeak — S
Black-headed Grosbeak — S
Blue Grosbeak — S
Lazuli Bunting — S
Indigo Bunting — S
Painted Bunting — S
Dickcissel — S
Olive Sparrow — R
Green-tailed Towhee — W
Rufous-sided Towhee — R

SPARROW, JUNCOES, AND
  LONGSPURS:
Botteri's Sparrow — S
Cassir's Sparrow — R
Rufous-crowned Sparrow — R
Chipping Sparrow — R
Clay-colored Sparrow — W
Field Sparrow — W
Vesper Sparrow — W
Lark Sparrow — R
Black-throated Sparrow — R
Lark Bunting — W
Savanah Sparrow — W
Grasshopper Sparrow — W
Henslow's Sparrow — W
Le Conte's Sparrow — W
Sharp-tailed Sparrow — W

Fox Sparrow — W
Song Sparrow — W
Lincoln's Sparrow — W
Swamp Sparrow — W
White-throated Sparrow — W
White-crowned Sparrow — W
Harris' Sparrow — W
Slate Colored Junco — W
McGown's Longspur — W
Chestnut-colored Longspur —
  W

MEADOWLARKS, BLACK-
  BIRDS, AND ORIOLES:
Bobolink — S
Red-winged Blackbird — R
Eastern Meadowlark — R
Western Meadowlark — W
Yellow-headed Blackbird — W
Rusty Blackbird — W
Brewer's Blackbird — W
Great-tailed Grackle — R
Boat-tailed Grackle — R
Common Grackle — W
Bronzed Cowbird — R
Brown-headed Cowbird — R
Orchard Oriole — S
Hooded Oriole — R

FINCHES:
Purple Finch — W
House Finch — R
Red Crossbill — W
Pine Siskin — W
Lesser Goldfinch — R
American Goldfinch — W
Evening Grosbeak — W

WEAVER FINCHES:
House Sparrow — R

Butterflies of the Coastal Bend:

Butterflies are important as they play a roll in pollena-
tion. In their larval state, as caterpillars, they may damage
garden flowers, vegetables, crops, and sometimes whole for-

171

ests. The following checklist is not a comprehensive one, but a mere few of the most common ones seen in this area.

monarch	sleepy orange
cloudless sulphur	southern skipperling
julie	giant swallowtail
white peacock	checkered white
question mark	alfalfa
dainty sulphur	American painted lady
polydamus swallowtail	little sulphur
great purple hairstreak	falcate orange tip
grey hairstreak	queen
tawny emperor	amymone
snout	orange barred sulphur
scudder's patched	Gulf fritillary
large orange sulphur	white striped long
buckeye	ceraunus blue
great southern white	lyside
red admiral	dog face
goatweek	pipe vine swallowtail

Shell List:

More than half the shells found in the Texas Coastal Bend shores are minute, needing a microscope or magnifying glass to identify them. This list names some of the more common larger shells found around our bays and gulf beaches:

Bay:

nerites	dwarf surf clam
hooked mussel	shark's eye
periwinkle	jackknife clam
bay scallop	Florida rock shell
wentletraps	stout tagelus
eastern oyster	dove shell
cerriths	cross-barred venus
buttercup lucina	lightning whelk
plicate horn shell	Texas quahog
thick lucina	striate bubble
slipper shell	Angel wing
	coffee melamphus

Gulf Beach:

sundial
tulip mussel
purple sea snail
sawtooth penshell
slippers shell
bay scallop
fighting conch
eastern oyster
shark's eye
broad ribbed candita
baby's ear
giant atlantic cockle
scotch bonnet
channeled duck clam

giant eastern murex
coquina shell
lightning whelk
alternate tellin
banded tulip shell
disk doscinia
lettered olive
southern quahog
Salle's auger
angel wing
striped false limpet
common spirula
mossy ark
sanddollar (not a shell)
other ark shells

Note: If you collect live shells please leave some to repopulate the area. If they are dead shells take as many as you need.

Sanddollars may be bleached in a small tray of diluted clorox. Leave in the direct sunlight for several hours, then rinse. They turn a bright snowy white.

To aid in your shell collecting and beachcombing efforts, you may like to learn more about it by reading some of these books: *Beachcombers' Guide to Gulf Coast Marinelife, Common Marine Invertebrates, Seashells of the Texas Coast.*

Please pay attention to winds, currents, seasons and tides. Low tides and different seasons produce an ever changing variety of sea drift to search through.

Wildflowers:

Anyone who is fortunate enough to see our masses of bluebonnets along the highways and byways will never forget them. They even inspired a song, "Bluebonnets of Texas." Quick thinking members of the Texas Chapter of Colonial Dames, who nominated the blossom for state flower, led to its selection. In 1901 the House of Representatives were debating several possibilities when "Cactus Jack" Garner made an eloquent and impassioned plea for his favorite, the cactus flower. Colonial Dames present in the House Chamber, sen-

173

sing defeat of their favorite, quickly countered with a painting of blue-bonnets, which some of the legislators had never seen. As they unveiled the picture, the House erupted in loud applause; and the bluebonnet became the official state flower by unanimous vote.

Texas is host to over 5,000 wildflower species. Each season offers its own specialty, but the springtime is particularly spectacular along the roadside shoulders where the highway department allows nature's handiwork to be undisturbed for a few short weeks. The bluebonnets, buttercups, and Indian paintbrushes drape the meadows and are well worth the drive to see. Photograph all you like, but please refrain from picking them so that others might enjoy them too.

Several publications are very beneficial for those interested in wildflowers: *Flora of the Coastal Bend,* by Fred Jones; *Roadside Flowers of Texas,* by Mary Motz Wills and Howard Irwin. Also a free folder of color photographs of the more predominant flowers may be obtained by writing P.O. Box 5064, Austin, Texas 78763 or by going by any Texas Tourist Bureau.

> Angel's trumpet: April–October
> Aster: October–November
> Ballmoss: June–August
> Bitterweed: April–December
> Bladderpod: February–April
> Bluebonnets: February–April
> Blue-eyed grass: March–May
> Broomwood: July–December
> Brown-eyed Susan: April–May
> Bull-nettle: March–November
> Butterfly Pea: March–November
> Century Plant, Agave: April–June

Coral Beans: March–June
Coreopsis: February–December
DAISIES:
Camphor Daisy: June–December
Cowpen Daisy: February–December
Fleabane Daisy: March–May
Lazy Daisy: March–June
Pincushion Daisy: March–June
Sleepy Daisy: April–December
DANDELION:
Dwarf Dandelion: July–November
Texas Dandelion: March–May
Day Flower: March–December
Dodder: May–September
Firewheel: March–September
Frogfruit: May–October
Gayfeather: September–November
Goldenrod: September–November
Indian Paintbrush: March–May
IRISES:
Celestial Iris: March–May
Goatfoot morning-glory: May–December
Golden-wave: February–December
Heart's Delight: February–May
Henbit: November–May
Ladies Tresses (our only orchid): April–June
Lantana: April–November
Leatherflower: March–October
Lemon Horsemint: April–June
LILIES:
Rain Lily: June–November
Spider Lily: March–May
Yellow Atamsco Lily: July–September
Lobellia: August–December
Locoweed: April–June
Marsh Fleabane: June–October
Mexican Hat: April–December
Milkweed: May–September
Mistletoe: October–March

175

Mustard: February–May
Nightshades: April–November
Old Man's Beard: May–September
Old-Plainsman: March–July
Partridge Pea: June–December
Phacelia: Feburary–April
Phlox: February–June
Prairie Larkspur: March–May
Primroses — pink, yellow: February–June — sparingly to December
Puccoon: March–April
Puffs of Pink: February–March
Ragwort: October–November
Railroad Vine: May–September
Rumex: March–October
Scarlet Salvia: April–November
Sea Lavender: May–November
Skullcap: February–November
Small Polkweed (rouge plant): was once crushed and used as rouge, hence its name. In fall its leaves turn pink.
Spanish Anemone: white to dark blue
Spanish Moss: May–June
Spiderwort: February–June
Sunflowers: March–December
Texas Bindweed: May–September
Texas Prickly Poppy: February–May
Thelesperma: March–November
THISTLES:
Bull-Thistle: March–June
Sow Thistle: January–December
Star Thistle: January–July
Texas Thistle: February–June
Toadflax: February–May
Turkscap: May–November
Venus' Looking-Glass: March–May
VERBESINA:
Cowpen Daisy: February–December
Frostweed: September–November

Verbena: March–November
Vine Snapdragon: April–December
Violet: February–March
Virginia Peppergrass: February–May
Wild Carrots: April–June
Wild Dewberry: March–May
Wild Honeysuckle: April–November
Wild Indigo: March–May
Wild Morninglory: May–September
Wild Onion: March–April
Wild Petunia: April–November
Wild Tobacco: March–December
Winecups: February–June
Wood Sorrels — yellow, pink: March–August
Yucca (also known as Spanish Dagger): January–April

Seashore Vegetation List:

Although Padre Island is a barrier island, and exists in a harsh environment, the vegetation here is plentiful. Listed below are the common names of the more recognized plants. They are found on the beach, the foredunes, the grassland plains, the pond and marsh sites, the dune fields, the tidal flats, and the spoil banks. Over 400 species, representing some 75 plant families, exist here. Only a few are named. This list is adapted from the Padre Island National Seashore list.

salt wort	smooth cordgrass
plains pricklypear	lazy daisy, white daisy
glass wort	sea purslane
Spanish dagger	spiny aster
sea oats	marsh hay cordgrass
sunrose	bull thistle
beach tea	whitestem wild indigo
yucca	Texas thistle
goatfoot morning glory	Gulf cordgrass
widow's tears	indian blanket, firewheel
bitter parnicum	sand burr
spiderwort	seashore phlox

black mangrove
pepperbark
false garlic
tickle-tongue
cudweed
beach gerardia
common sunflower
prairie gerardia
silverleaf sunflower
saltmarsh gerardia
brown-eyed susan
toadflax
sweet goldenrod
bird pepper, chilipiquin
seacost goldenrod
salt cedar
saltmarsh morning glory
common cat-tail
peppergrass

rattle pod
live oak
coral bean
big bluestem
retama, paloverde
beardgrass, bushy bluestem
honey mesquite
splitbeard bluestem
evening primrose
seashore saltgrass
beach evening primrose
sweetbay
wood-sorrel
huisache
prickly poppy
eastern pricklypear
sea lavender
Texas pricklypear
annual phlox
pinweed

Education in the Coastal Bend:

Bee County College — Junior College — 3800 Charco Road, Beeville, Texas 78102 — (512) 358-3130.

Corpus Christi State University — Presently an upper level university. Will become a full-fledged part of the Texas A&M system in 1994. 6300 Ocean Dr. 78412 — (512) 994-9624.

Del Mar College — Junior College, Baldwin at Ayers, Corpus Christi, Texas 78404 — (512) 881-8200.

Texas A&I — A four year and graduate level university, Kingsville, Texas — (512) 595-2111.

Victoria County Junior College — 2200 East Red River, 77901 (512) 573-3291.

Bibliography

Adams, Audrey. *Karankawa Boy*. San Antonio, Texas: The Naylor Company, 1965.

Alexander, D. B. and T. Webb. *Texas Homes of the 19th Century*. Austin, Texas: University of Texas Press, 1966.

Anderson, E. *Boss Rule in South Texas The Progressive Era*. Austin, Texas: University of Texas Press, 1982.

Andrews, J. *Seashells of the Texas Coast*. Austin, Texas: University of Texas Press, 1975.

———. *Texas Bluebonnets*. Austin, Texas: University of Texas Press, 1986.

———. *Texas Shells*. Austin, Texas: University of Texas Press, 1981.

Ashford, G. *Spanish Texas: Yesterday and Today*. Austin, Texas: Jenkins Press, 1971.

Baxter, David. *Texas Wildlife: Photographs from Texas Parks and Wildlife Magazine*. College Station, Texas: Texas A & M University Press, 1978.

Becker, A. C. *Fishing the Texas Coast, Inshore and Offshore*. Houston, Texas: Cordovan Corporation, 1975.

Bedichek, R. *Adventures With a Texas Naturalist*. Austin, Texas: University of Texas Press, 1961.

———. *Karankawa Country*. Austin, Texas: University of Texas Press, 1950.

Bomar, B. W. *Texas Weather*. Austin, Texas: University of Texas Press, 1983.

Briscoe, E. R. *City by the Sea: A History of Corpus Christi, Texas 1519–1875*. New York: Vantage Press, 1985.

The Building of Corpus Christi. Corpus Christi, Texas: Charter Savings and Loan Association.

Connor, V. L. *Treasures Recovered Off Padre Island*. J. A. Baldwin Co., 1969.

Cornelius, S. *An Ecological Survey of Alazan Bay, Texas*. Vol. 1 LC 83-71623. C. K. Wildlife Res., 1984.

179

Corpus Christi, Texas — 100 Years. Corpus Christi, Texas: *Corpus Christi Caller Times,* 1952.

Crenshaw, T. C. *Texas Blackland Heritage.* Waco, Texas: Texian Press.

Crofford, Lena H. *Pioneers on the Nueces.* San Antonio, Texas: The Naylor Company, 1963.

Crombey, M. and M. Nutting. *Rock Hunting in Texas — Where to go and How to get There.* Houston, Texas: Gulf Publishing Company, 1936.

Davis, J. L. *Treasure, People, Ships and Dreams.* Austin, Texas: Texas Antiquities Committee, 1977.

Davis, W. B. *The Mammals of Texas.* Austin, Texas: Texas Parks & Wildlife Department, 1974.

De La Pena, J. E. *With Santa Anna in Texas: A Personal Narrative of the Revolution.* College Station, Texas: Texas A&M University Press.

Dixon, J. R. *Amphibians and Reptiles of Texas.* College Station, Texas: Texas A&M Press, 1987.

Dobie, J. F. *Cow People.* Austin Texas: University of Texas Press, 1981.

———. *The Flavor of Texas.* Austin, Texas: Jenkins, 1975.

———. *Legends of Texas, Vol. 1 Lost Mines and Buried Treasures, Vol. 2. Pirate's Gold and Other Tales.* Hatboro, Louisiana: Folklore Association, 1964.

———. *The Longhorns.* New York: Bramhall House, 1951.

———. *A Vaquero of the Brush Country.* Austin, Texas: University of Texas Press, 1981.

Dooley, Claude W. *Why Stop?* Odessa, Texas: Lone Star Legends Company, 1978.

Douglas, C. L. *Thunder on the Gulf.* Fort Collins, Colorado: Old Army Press, 1973.

Durham, G. *Taming the Nueces Strip: The Story of McNelly's Rangers.* Austin, Texas: University of Texas Press, 1962.

Eisenhauer, A. and G. Starnes. *Corpus Christi, Texas, A Picture Postcard History.* Corpus Christi, Texas: Anita's Antiques, 1987.

Farley, B. *How to Catch Fish in the Gulf of Mexico.* Corpus Christi, Texas: Texas News Syndicated Press, 1965.

Fotheringham, N., S. Brunenmeister, and P. Menefee. *Beachcomber's Guide to Gulf Coast Marine Life.* Houston, Texas: Lone Star Books, 1980.

Fotheringham, N. and S. Brunenmeister. *Common Marine Invertebrates.* Houston, Texas: Gulf Publishing Company, 1975.

Frissell, Toni. *The King Ranch, 1939–1944 — A Photographic Essay.* Dobbs Ferry, New York: Morgan and Morgan, 1975.

Frost, D. *The King Ranch Papers: An Unauthorized and Irreverent History of the World's Largest Landowners: Kleberg Family.* Chicago, Illinois: Aquarius Rising Production, 1985.

Girard, R. M. *Texas Rocks and Minerals — An Amateur's Guide.* Bureau of Economic Geology. Austin, Texas: University of Texas Press, 1964.

Gould, F. W. and T. W. Box. *Grasses of the Texas Coastal Bend.* College Station, Texas: Texas A&M University Press, 1965.

Gromberg, M. and L. Nutting. *Rock Hunting in Texas — Where to go and What to Look For.* Houston, Texas: Gulf Publishing Company, 1986.

Guthrie, Keith. *History of San Patricio County.* Austin, Texas: Nortex Press, 1986.

Hale, L. and A. Holmes. *The Texas Gulf Coast: Interpretations by Nine Artists.* College Station, Texas: Texas A&M University Press, 1979.

Haley, J. E. *Charles Goodnight: Cowman and Plainsman.* Oklahoma City, Oklahoma: University of Oklahoma Press, 1981.

Ham, H. *South Texas Wildflowers.* Kingsville, Texas: Conner Museum Publication: Texas A&I University, 1984.

Haragan, D. R. *Blue Northers to Sea Breezes: Texas Weather and Climate.* Dallas, Texas: Hendrick-Long, 1983.

Hebert, R. B. *The Forgotten Colony: San Patricio de Hibernia.* Austin, Texas: Eakin Publications, 1981.

Hester, T. R. *Digging into South Texas Prehistory.* San Antonio, Texas: Corona Publishing, 1980.

Hiller, I. *Young Naturalist.* College Station, Texas: Texas A&M University Press, 1983.

The History of Nueces County. Austin, Texas: Jenkins Publishing Company, 1972.

The History of Refugio Co., Texas. Dallas, Texas: Curtis Media Corporation, 1985. Refugio Co. History Book Committee National Share Graphics.

Hoese, H. D., R. H. Moore and V. F. Sonnier. *Fishes of the Gulf of Mexico: Texas, Louisiana, and Adjacent Waters.* College Station, Texas: Texas A&M University Press, 1977. Illustrations by Dinah Bowman.

Husak, A. *Fishing the Bays of Texas.* Houston, Texas: Cordovan Corporation, 1974.

———. *The Saltwater Craftsman.* Houston, Texas: Cordovan Corporation, 1976.

The Indian Years. Living with the Texas Past. Series #1. Austin, Texas: Texas Historical Commission, 1983.

Irwin, Howard S. *Roadside Flowers of Texas.* Austin, Texas: University of Texas Press, 1961.

Jackson, J. *Los Mestenos: Spanish Ranching in Texas, 1721–1821.* College Station, Texas: Texas A&M Press.

Jones, F. B. *Flora of the Texas Coastal Bend.* Corpus Christi, Texas: Mission Press, 1975.

Jordan, T. G. *Texas Graveyards: A Cultural Legacy.* Austin, Texas: University of Texas Press, 1984.

Kelly, Thomas C. *An Archaeological Survey of Portions of Mud and St. Joseph Islands.* San Antonio, Texas: University of Texas at San Antonio Center for Archaeological Research, 1980.

Kirkley, G. *A Guide to Texas Rivers and Streams.* Houston, Texas: Gulf Publication Company, 1983.

Kutac, E. A. *Texas Birds — Where They Are and How to Find Them.* Houston, Texas: Gulf Publishing Company, 1982.

Lasater, D. Falfurrias. *Ed C. Lasater and the Development of South Texas.* College Station, Texas: Texas A&M University Press, 1985.

Legends of Texas, Vol. 1 Lost Mines and Buried Treasures, Vol. 2 Pirates Gold and Other Tales. Gretna, Louisiana: Pelican Publishing.

Little, M. J. *Camper's Guide to Texas Parks, Lakes, and Forests.* Houston, Texas: Gulf Publishing Company, 1983.

Loughmiller, C. and L. *Texas Wildflowers, A Field Guide.* Austin, Texas: University of Texas Press, 1984.

Madsen, William. *The Mexican Americans of South Texas.* New York: Holt, Rinehart and Winston, Inc., 1973.

Malsch, Brownson. *Indianola, The Mother of Western Texas.* Austin, Texas: State House Press, 1988.

Maril, R. L. *Texas Shrimpers.* College Station, Texas: Texas A&M Press, 1983.

Martin, G. C. *Indian Tribes of the Mission Nuestra Senora del Refugio.* Corpus Christi, Texas: Bootstraps Press, 1972.

Matthews, W. H. III. *Texas Fossils — An Amateur Collector's Handbook.* Austin, Texas: Texas University Press, 1960.

McAlister, W. H. and M. K. McAlister. *Guidebook to the Aransas National Wildlife Refuge.* Victoria, Texas: Mince County Press, 1987.

McCarty, F. M. *Texas Guidebook: Howard's Original.* 5th Edition.

McCracken, K. H. *Connie Hagar — The Life History of a Texas Bird Watcher.* College Station, Texas: Texas A&M University Press, 1986.

McDonald, A. P. *The Trail to San Jacinto.* American Press, 1982.

McIlvain, M. H. *Texas Auto Trails: The South and The Rio Grande Valley.* Austin, Texas: University of Texas Press, 1985.

Miller, G. and D. Tull. *Texas Parks and Campgrounds: A Vacation Guide to North, East, and the Coastal Texas*. Austin, Texas: Texas Monthly Press, 1984.

Miller, S. *Itinerant Photographer — Corpus Christi, 1934*. Santa Fe, New Mexico: University of New Mexico Press, 1987.

Newcomb, W. W., Jr. *The Indians of Texas, From Prehistoric to Modern Times*. Austin, Texas: University of Texas Press, 1961.

Olds, D. L. *Texas Legacy from the Gulf — Report on 16th Century Shipwreck Materials Recovered from the Texas Tidelands*. Austin, Texas: Texas Memorial Museum Miscellaneous Papers #5, 1976.

Parker, A. L. *The Coastal Bend — A Pictorial History*. Corpus Christi, Texas: South Coast Publishing Company, 1986.

———. *Discovery Book for the Texas Coast*. Corpus Christi, Texas: South Coast Publishing Company, 1986.

Peterson, R. T. *A Field Guide to the Birds of Texas and Adjacent States*. Boston: Houghton, Mifflin Co., 1960.

Pruett, J. L. and E. B. Cole. *Goliad Massacre: A Tragedy of the Texas Revolution*. Austin, Texas: Eakin Publications, 1985.

Rappole, J. H. and G. W. Blacklock. *Birds of Texas Coastal Bend, Abundance and Distribution*. College Station, Texas: Texas A&M University Press, 1985.

Rayburn, J. C. et al. *Century of Conflict, 1821–1913: Incidents in the Lives of William Neale and William A. Neale, Early Settlers in South Texas*. Salem, NH: Ayer Co. Publishing, 1976.

Renfro, H. B. *Geological Highway Map of Texas*. Tulsa, Oklahoma: American Association of Petroleum Geologists.

Roads of Texas. Fredericksburg, Texas: Shearer Publications, 1988.

Robertson, Brian. *Wild Horse Desert. The Heritage of South Texas*. Edinburg, Texas: New Santander Press, 1985.

Ruff, A. *The Best of Texas Festivals*. Houston, Texas: Gulf Publishing Company, 1986.

Sheldon, R. A. *Roadside Geology of Texas*. Missoula, Montana: Mountain Press Publishing Co., 1979.

Smith, G., Jr. *Forgotten Texas*. Austin, Texas: Texas Monthly Press, 1983.

Smith, T. *Images of Rural Texas*. Wichita Falls, Texas: Red River Pub.

Smylie, V. *Conquistadores and Cannibals*. Corpus Christi, Texas: Texas News Syndicated Press, 1964.

———. *The Secrets of Padre Island — An Informal History of America's Most Fascinating Island*. Corpus Christi, Texas: Texas News Syndicated Press, 1972.

———. *Taming of the Texas Coast*. Corpus Christi, Texas: Texas News Syndicated Press, 1965.

Stephens, A. Ray. *The Taft Ranch*. Austin, Texas: The University of Texas Press, 1964.

Suter, H. A. *A Voice of Reason — Environmental Insights*. Corpus Christi, Texas: Audubon Outdoor Club, 1986.

Syers, W. F. *Backroads of Texas*. Houston, Texas: Gulf Publishing Company, 1979.

Texas Forest Service. *Famous Trees of Texas*. College Station, Texas: Texas A&M University Press, 1970.

Thompson, E. *Caldo Largo*. New York: G. P. Putnam's and Sons, 1976.

Tinsley, R. *Fishing Texas*. Fredericksburg, Texas: Shearer Publications, 1988.

Torres, E. *Green Medicine — Traditional Mexican — American Herbal Remedies*. Kingsville, Texas: Nieves Press.

Townsend, T. *Texas Treasure Coast*. Austin, Texas: Eakin Publications, 1980.

Turner, E. S. and T. R. Hester. *A Field Guide to Stone Artifacts of Texas Indians*. Austin, Texas: Texas Monthly Press, 1985.

Tveten, J. C. *Coastal Texas: Water, Land and Wildlife*. College Station, Texas: Texas A&M University Press, 1982.

Tyler, P. E. and R. Tyler. *Texas Museums: A Guide Book*. Austin, Texas: University of Texas Press, 1983.

Veach, J. W. and D. Veach. *The Sanddollar Book*. Port Isabel, Texas: Sanddollar News Service, 1977.

Walraven, B. *Corpus Christi — The History of a Texas Seaport*. Woodland Hills, California: Windsor Publishing, 1982.

Warren, Betsy. *Indians Who Lived in Texas*. Dallas, Texas: Hendrick-Long Publishing Company, 1981.

Watson, M. G. and A. Lillico. *Taft Ranch*. Taft, Texas: Texas Blackland Museum, 1980.

Weddle, R. S. *LaSalle, the Mississippi of the Gulf*. College Station, Texas: Texas A&M University Press, 1987.

———. *Spanish Sea — The Gulf of Mexico in North American Discovery*. College Station, Texas: Texas A&M University Press, 1985.

Weems, J. F. *The Story of Texas — 4 Parts*. Fredericksburg, Texas: Shearer Publications, 1986.

Weise, B. R. and W. A. White. *Padre Island National Seashore, A Guide to the Geology, Natural Environments, and History of a Texas Barrier Island*. Austin, Texas: University of Texas Press, 1980.

Williams, D. *South Plains: A Pictorial History of 28 Texas Counties*. Ellyn Illinois: Paramount, Texas, 1988.

Williams, J. W. *The Big Ranch Country*. Austin, Texas: Eakin Publications, 1968.

Williams, L. W. *Ranches and Ranching in Spanish Texas*. Boston: American Press, 1982.

Wills, M. M. *Roadside Flowers of Texas*. Austin, Texas: University of Texas Press, 1961.

Wootters, J. A *Guide to Hunting in Texas*. Houston, Texas: Gulf Publishing Company, 1979.

Woodey, B. and S. Hagler. *Where Texas Meets the Sea: A Coastal Portrait*. Dallas, Texas: Presswords, 1985.

Wyatt, E. *The Building of Corpus Christi*. Corpus Christi, Texas: Charter Savings and Loan Association, 1977.

The Years of Exploration. *Living with the Texas Past*. Series #3. Austin, Texas: Texas Historical Commission, 1984.